Rereading Marx in the A

Rereading Marx in the Age of Digital Capitalism

Christian Fuchs

PLUTO  PRESS

First published 2019 by Pluto Press
345 Archway Road, London N6 5AA

www.plutobooks.com

British Library Cataloguing in Publication Data
A catalogue record for this book is available from the British Library

ISBN   978 0 7453 4000 5   Hardback
ISBN   978 0 7453 3999 3   Paperback
ISBN   978 1 7868 0517 1   PDF eBook
ISBN   978 1 7868 0519 5   Kindle eBook
ISBN   978 1 7868 0518 8   EPUB eBook

This book is printed on paper suitable for recycling and made from fully
managed and sustained forest sources. Logging, pulping and manufacturing
processes are expected to conform to the environmental standards of the
country of origin.

Typeset by Stanford DTP Services, Northampton, England

This book is dedicated to my son Luca Sandoval-Fuchs who like all babies, toddlers and children of the world symbolises the light of socialism.

Contents

Acknowledgements

An earlier version of Chapter 2 was first published in *Capital & Class*: Fuchs, Christian. 2016. Marx's *Capital* in the Information Age. *Capital & Class* 41 (1): 51–67. http://journals.sagepub.com/doi/full/10.1177/0309816816678573

Chapter 4 was first published in 2018 under the title 'Karl Marx & Communication @ 200: Towards a Marxian Theory of Communication' in the journal *tripleC: Communication, Capitalism & Critique* (www.triple-c.at), Volume 16, No. 2.

A shorter version of Chapter 5 was first published in 2018 under the title 'Repeating Marxian Analysis in Digital Capitalism: The Case of Industry 4.0 and the Industrial Internet as the Digital German Ideology' in the journal *tripleC: Communication, Capitalism & Critique* (www.triple-c.at), Volume 16, No. 1.

Chapter 6 was first published in 2017 under the title 'Reflections on Michael Hardt and Antonio Negri's Book "Assembly"' in the journal *tripleC: Communication, Capitalism & Critique* (www.triple-c.at), Volume 15, No. 2.

All of these chapters are reproduced with permission by the publishers.

1

Introduction: Rereading Marx in the Age of Digital Capitalism

The year 2017 marked the 150th anniversary of the publication of Volume 1 of Marx's *Capital* and 5 May 2018 was Karl Marx's bicentenary. After decades of marginalisation, we today find a repeated interest in Karl Marx's work. This book asks the questions: Why is Marx relevant today? How can we make sense of Marx in the age of digital and communicative capitalism?

To reread something should include that we remember something, re-say and re-voice it, do something again, and struggle for something again. Rereading Marx means remembering Marx's works, re-voicing and re-saying Marx's ideas and politics, re-doing his critique, and repeating the struggle against capitalism and for socialism. To re-do something is never a mechanical mapping or reflection, but rather a creative dialectical process of sublation that preserves, eliminates and creates something novel. To reread Marx is not a mapping of Marx, but a creative renewal of Marx's analysis and radical politics in the twenty-first century.

With works such as *Capital, Grundrisse, Economic & Philosophic Manuscripts, The German Ideology, The Communist Manifesto, Class Struggles in France, The 18th Brumaire of Louis Bonaparte, Contribution to Critique of Political Economy, The Civil War in France, Theories of Surplus Value*, etc., Marx laid the foundations for the critique of capitalism's political economy. The approach he advanced operates with the help of categories such as the commodity, work, labour, exchange-value, use-value, value, the labour theory of value, labour-time, abstract and concrete labour, money, capital, capitalism, wages, prices, profits, fetishism, surplus-value, necessary labour, surplus labour, class, exploitation, alienation, accumulation, profit, ideology, absolute and relative surplus-value production, formal and real subsumption, co-operation, machinery, the means of production, the general intellect, the means of communication, the collective worker, the rate of surplus-value, the organic composition of capital, the rate of profit, the international division of labour, primitive accumulation, the antagonism of productive forces and relations of production, modes of production, capitalist crises, overaccumulation, the tendency of the profit rate to fall, the anarchy of the market, overproduction, underconsumption, profit-squeeze, devaluation, fictitious capital, rent, landed property, transportation, the world market, uneven geographical development, global capital, colonialism, imperialism, interest, credit, the historical tendency of capitalist accumulation, circulation, reproduction, consumption, distribution, merchant's capital, department I & II of social production, the state, species-being, Bonapartism, materialism, the dialectic, contradictions, class struggles, class consciousness, realm of necessity, realm of freedom, the commons, communism, socialism, etc.

Taken together, these categories form the foundations of a critical theory of capitalism and of its economic system, political system, cultural system, its technological paradigms, the human/nature relationship within capitalism, and aspects of subject/object, time and space in capitalism. Marx's approach is inherently critical, which means that it analyses capitalism's contradictions, its crisis tendencies, struggles and the foundation of alternatives to capitalism as the determinate negation of capitalism. Two hundred years of the development of Marxian theory have resulted in numerous approaches, strands, interpretations, debates and conflicts.

The rise of neoliberal capitalism in society, of postmodernism in culture and academia, and of identity politics has together with the collapse of the Soviet system, the degenerations brought about by various forms of Stalinism, and the neoliberalisation of social democracy resulted in a decline of Marxian-inspired theory and praxis during the past decades. Francis Fukuyama was therefore able to postulate in 1992 that the end of history had arrived and to claim that capitalism and liberal democracy would exist forever. Many academics in the social sciences and humanities to a certain extent have practised Fukuyamaism by forgetting about capitalism and the analysis of society's totality. They have instead focused on micro-analysis, postmodernism, the attack on 'grand narratives' and truth claims, and categories such as globalisation, individualisation, risk, networks, modernity, identity, etc. While Marx has increasingly become absent in theory and praxis, the class contradiction and inequalities have expanded so that he has in light of his absence paradoxically become more needed than ever before.

Twenty-five years later, societies and sociology have changed. The notion of capitalism has in the light of capitalism's actual crisis made a return into the public and sociological vocabulary. A new world economic crisis emerged in 2008. It turned in many parts of the world into a political, social, austerity, ideological and legitimacy crisis of capitalist society as well as into the rise of new nationalisms and authoritarian forms of capitalism (Fuchs 2018). Marx keeps on haunting capitalism in the twenty-first century. Talking about Marx means talking about class, capitalism, crisis and alternatives to capitalism. It is therefore evident that Marx will remain our contemporary as long as capitalism continues to exist. The time has come to repeat Marx.

In contemporary capitalism, knowledge labour, digital communication technologies and information commodities play a significant role. One can therefore speak of digital capitalism or communicative capitalism as an important dimension of capitalism today. It is not the only dimension of capitalism because we also live simultaneously in finance capitalism, hyper-industrial capitalism, crisis capitalism, authoritarian capitalism, neoliberal capitalism, mobility capitalism, global capitalism, etc. All of these dimensions interact. This book gives particular attention to the relevance of Marx in the context of digital and communicative capitalism today.

Whereas in the 1990s and the first decade of the 2000s, it was difficult to talk about Marx without immediately being confronted with the prejudices against Marx (see Eagleton 2011) so that a discussion about Marx and the critique of capitalism could not even be started, today there is more willingness to listen to what Marxist theory has to say. In the age where neoliberal capitalism is in deep political, economic and ideological crisis and tends to turn into new authoritarian capitalisms, it has not just become evident that the market and the commodity form cannot solve human problems, but also the time has come to once again take Marx and socialism seriously.

Facing economic, political and ideological crises, we have to reread and repeat Marx today. Rereading and repeating Marx does not mean to mechanically apply Marx's thought to twenty-first-century society. It also does not mean to treat his writings as scriptures, from which one repeats one and the same quotations over and over again.

First, to reread and repeat Marx today means to develop analyses and critiques of class and capitalism in the twenty-first century in a historical and dialectical manner. It means to study how capitalism not just as economic formation, but as societal formation is transforming and damaging human lives, society and nature. It means repeating Marx's categories – such as the commodity, labour, value, surplus-value class, exploitation, capital, exploitation, domination, ideology, class struggles, means/relations/modes of production, means of communication, the general intellect, communism, etc. – in the twenty-first century. Marx was both a historical and a dialectical thinker. To repeat Marx in the twenty-first century, therefore, neither means to abolish his approach, theory and politics, nor to completely re-invent them, nor to leave them unchanged. That capitalism is a historical and dialectical system means that it changes through crises in order to remain the same system of exploitation. To reread and repeat Marx therefore means to *sublate* Marx's categories based on a dialectic of continuity and change. Whereas postmodernists have preached for decades that society has completely changed, orthodox social theorists claim that nothing at all has changed. Postmodernism is almost dead and overestimates change. The orthodoxy that nothing ever changes in contrast overestimates continuity.

Second, the contemporary capitalist age is profoundly ideological. To understand and change society, we therefore need to reread and repeat Marx's ideology critique. Through consumer culture and neoliberalism, we have experienced the commodification of (almost) everything and the constant presence of ideologies that justify commodity logic in all realms of everyday life. Commodity fetishism as ideology immanent to capital itself has thereby become universal. Rising inequalities have resulted in the intensification and extension of ideologies that distract attention from capitalist society as the underlying cause of social problems. The most evident form of political fetishism has in recent times been the rise of new political nationalisms.

Third, to reread and repeat Marx today means to envision and struggle for alternatives to capitalism. Marx stresses that history is not pre-determined and that humans make their own history. Even in dark times, it is never too late. And it is especially in such times important to envision alternatives and think of and work towards ways of how the gap between what could be and what is can be overcome. Capitalism is not the end of history. In order to humanise society, fundamental societal change is needed.

This book rereads and repeats Marx in the age of digital and communicative capitalism in six steps. Each step is organised as one chapter. To repeat Marx means to reread and reinterpret his major works today.

Chapter 2 – 'Rereading Marx's Capital in the Information Age' – presents foundations of repeating Marx by reading *Capital* in the information age. Repeating Marx requires that we reconstruct the history of his theory and concepts. Chapters 3 and 4 repeat Marx by reconstructing his concepts of technology/machinery (Chapter 3: 'Rereading Marx as Critical Sociologist of Technology') as well as communication (Chapter 4: 'Rereading Karl Marx as Critical Theorist of Communication'). Rereading and repeating Marx also means to update, develop and apply his approach to contemporary phenomena. Chapter 5 – 'Rereading Marx in the Age of Digital Capitalism: The Case of Industry 4.0 and the Industrial Internet as the Digital German Ideology' – rereads and repeats Marx by updating his critique in the age of digital capitalism as the critique of the concept of industry 4.0/the industrial Internet.

Rereading and repeating Marx also means to repeat and remake socialist praxis, that is, emancipatory politics that aim at the establishment of a participatory society of the commons. Chapter 6 – Rereading Marx in the Age of Digital Capitalism: Reflections on Michael Hardt and Antonio Negri's Book *Assembly* – reflects on repeating Marx's socialist praxis via an engagement with Michael Hardt and Toni Negri's book *Assembly* that aims at inspiring contemporary political struggles. Chapter 7 provides some concluding thoughts.

To repeat Marx today means to recollect, reconstruct, retell, reread, reinterpret, renew, recast, revitalise, rethink, update, develop, apply, remake and redo Marxian theory and politics. Marx will keep on haunting capitalism as long as this system continues to exist. We need to repeat Marx today in order to stop capitalism's constant destructive repetition.

2

Rereading Marx's *Capital* in the Information Age

2.1 INTRODUCTION

The general interest in Marx's works has since the start of the new world economic crisis in 2008 significantly increased. Whereas before it was easier to dismiss the relevance of capitalism and class, their crucial relevance can hardly be ignored today. In this situation also the question arises of how to read Marx. This concerns especially Marx's most widely read book, *Capital Volume 1* that the United Nations Educational, Scientific and Cultural Organization (UNESCO) together with the *Communist Manifesto* inscribed on the Memory of the World Register in 2013. Whereas the German edition of *Capital* that the publisher Dietz distributes as part of the Marx Engels Works (MEW) had annually sold around 500–750 copies in the years 1990–2007, this number increased to 5,000 in 2008 and stands now regularly at about 1,500–2,000 (Meisner 2013). In times of digital capitalism, in which billions use Facebook, Google, Twitter, Weibo, iPhones, Spotify, online banking, online news sites and other media at work, in politics and everyday life, the time has come to read Marx's *Capital* from a media and communication studies perspective.

2.2 READING MARX'S *CAPITAL VOLUME 1* IN THE INFORMATION AGE

One can wonder how important media and the Internet are today and whether a media and communications-oriented reading of Marx's *Capital Volume 1*, as offered in the book *Reading Marx in the Information Age: A Media and Communication Studies Perspective on Capital Volume 1* (Fuchs 2016d), is really justified. Often it is claimed that all this talk about the digital and media revolution is a pure ideology that wants to convince us that we have entered an information society that has substituted capitalism.

In the 2015 Forbes list of the world's largest 2,000 transnational corporations (TNCs), one can find a total of 243 information companies, which amounts to 12 per cent. They are located in the sectors of advertising, broadcasting and cable, communications equipment, computer and electronic retail, computer hardware, computer services, computer storage devices, consumer electronics, electronics, Internet and catalogue retail, printing and publishing, semiconductors, software and programming, and telecommunications services. The information economy constitutes a significantly sized part of global capitalism. But in the same list, one finds, for example, 308 banks (15 per cent) that account for the majority of the 2,000 largest TNCs' capital assets. So one can easily argue that more than a media and communication studies perspective, we need a companion with the title *Reading Marx's Capital Volume 1 in the Financial Age*. Capitalism is, however, not homogeneous, but a differentiated dialectical unity of diverse capitalisms. We do not have to decide between information capitalism or finance capitalism (or other capitalisms, such as hyper-industrial capitalism, mobile capitalism, etc.), but rather have to see capitalism's manifold dimensions that mutually encroach each other (Fuchs 2014a: chapter 5). The information economy is itself highly financialised as, for example, the 2000 dot-com crisis and the constant flows of venture capitalism into Silicon Valley show. And information technology is one of the drivers of financialisation, as indicated by algorithmic trading, credit scoring algorithms or digital currencies such as Bitcoin. The computer is a universal machine that as networked information technology has affected all realms of everyday life, not just industry, labour and the economy. It is a convergence technology that has together with other societal developments advanced social convergence tendencies of culture and the economy, work time and leisure time, the home and the office, consumption and production, productive and unproductive labour, the public and the private (Fuchs 2015b). Reading *Capital* from an information perspective can therefore not be limited to the realm of media technologies and media content, but has to be extended to communication in society at large.

2.3 COMMUNICATION(S): STILL THE BLIND SPOT OF MARXIST THEORY

It is a positive development that media and cultural theorists have recently published books that remind us of the importance of Marx's works (see, e.g., Eagleton 2011; Fornäs 2013; Fuchs 2014a; Jameson 2011). Terry Eagleton (2011) in his book *Why Marx Was Right* deconstructs ten common myths and prejudices about Marx. He concludes:

> Marx saw socialism as a deepening of democracy, not as the enemy of it. ... There has been no more staunch champion of women's emancipation, world peace, the fight against fascism or the struggle for colonial freedom than the political movement to which his work gave birth. Was ever a thinker so travestied? (Eagleton 2011: 238–9)

In a time of high unemployment and high levels of precarious work, especially among young people, Frederic Jameson argues in his book *Representing Capital: A Reading of Volume One* that *Capital* 'is not a book about politics, and not even a book about labor, it is a book about unemployment' (Jameson 2011: 2). He concludes that Marx today helps us to 'be recommitted to the invention of a new kind of transformatory politics on a global scale' (Jameson 2011: 151). The Marxist cultural analysis of both Eagleton and Jameson has predominantly focused on literature. They have not much engaged in the analysis of other popular forms of culture and mediated culture, that is, the media's role in society. Eagleton (2013) has explicitly written about the fact that he does not use e-mail and the Internet:

> I shall soon be the only EMV (email virgin) left in the country. I have never sent an email, though I've occasionally cheated and asked my teenage son to do so for me. Nor have I ever used the internet. ... In my view, the internet is really an anti-modern device for slowing us all down, returning us to the rhythms of an earlier, more sedate civilization.

Johan Fornäs, a Swedish media and cultural studies scholar, has in contrast to Eagleton and Jameson analysed youth cultures, music scenes, and other forms of popular and mediated culture. Like Jameson and Eagleton, he has recently published a book about Marx: *Capitalism: A Companion to Marx's Economy Critique* provides an introduction to all three volumes of *Capital*. Fornäs concludes: 'Marx's dialectical critique of commodity fetishism and capitalist class relations remains a prime model for also understanding other late-modern contradictions in social life' (Fornäs 2013: 306; for a detailed discussion of Fornäs' book, see Fuchs 2013). It is an important development that media and cultural analysts write books about Marx and remind us of the importance of his works. It is, however, also a bit surprising that Jameson, Eagleton and Fornäs in these books do not profoundly draw on their knowledge about media and culture. All three books are rather general introductions to or interpretations of Marx's critique of the political economy, which creates the impression that the economy and culture are independent realms.

There remains a need for reading Marx from a media, communication and cultural studies perspective, which can help us to better understand the dialectic of culture and the economy: Culture and economy are identical and non-identical at the same time. All culture is produced in specific work processes. But culture is not just an economic phenomenon, but has emergent qualities; its meanings take effect all over society.

The dimensions of media, communication, culture, the digital and the Internet are often not taken seriously enough in Marxist theory, although they are significant phenomena of contemporary capitalism. In Marxist volumes, companions, journals, conferences, panels and keynote talks, such issues often feature not at all, rarely or only as exceptions from the rule that they are ignored. As an example: The titles of articles published in the journal *Historical Materialism* in the years 2006–14 mentioned communication-related keywords[1] only three times. This situation is certainly slowly changing, but there is still some way to go until the majority of Marxist theorists consider communication no longer as a superstructure and secondary. Raymond Williams' insight that 'modes of consciousness', such as language, information, communication, art and popular culture, 'are material' (Williams 1977: 190) has thus far not adequately diffused into Marxist theory. Dallas W. Smythe, who developed the first political economy of communication university module in the late 1940s, argued in 1977, the same year as Raymond Williams published *Marxism and Literature*, that the 'media of communications and related institutions' represent 'a blindspot in Marxist theory' (Smythe 1977: 1). Almost 40 years later, the situation has not fundamentally changed.

2.4 THE POLITICAL ECONOMY OF COMMUNICATION

There is, however, a longer tradition of Marxist political economy of communication that has established itself within the academic field of media

---

1   Communication, communications, computer, cyberspace, digital, ICT, ICTs, information, Internet, media, web, WWW.

and communication studies along with textbooks (Hardy 2014; Mosco 2009), institutions such as the International Association of Media and Communication Research's Political Economy of Communication Sections (www.iamcr.org/s-wg/section/political-economy-section), handbooks (Wasko et al. 2011), collections (Fuchs & Mosco 2012; Golding & Murdock 1997; Mattelart & Siegelaub 1979, 1983), as well as journals such as *tripleC: Communication, Capitalism & Critique* (www. triple-c.at) or *The Political Economy of Communication* (www.polecom. org).

The political economist of communication Janet Wasko (2014: 261) concludes in a review of the field's development in the twenty-first century: 'Studying the political economy of communications is no longer a marginal approach to media and communication studies in many parts of the world.' Marxism has after many decades had an important impact on the field of media and communication studies, which is good news. The bad news is, however, that this circumstance has hardly been recognised and acknowledged within Marxist theory at large. Whereas Marxist theorists' works are regularly read, cited and applied by Marxist communication scholars, the opposite is not true. I want to illustrate this fact with an example.

In Britain, Marxist political economy of media, communication and culture goes back to a seminal article by Graham Murdock and Peter Golding published in 1973. They defined as the starting point for such analyses 'the recognition that the mass media are first and foremost industrial and commercial organizations which produce and distribute commodities' (Murdock & Golding 1973: 205–6). They stress that the media 'also disseminate ideas about economic and political structures. It is this second and ideological dimension of mass media production which gives it its importance and centrality and which requires an approach in terms of not only economics but also politics' (Murdock & Golding 1973: 206–7).

In 2013, 40 years later, Ngai-Ling Sum and Bob Jessop (2013) published the book *Towards a Cultural Political Economy: Putting Culture in its Place in Political Economy*. It aims to introduce culture to political economy approaches such as the Regulation School that has tradition-ally ignored this dimension of society and focused on the interaction of regimes of accumulation and modes of regulation. The book is therefore part of a project to go beyond the regulation approach. The two authors completely ignore and do not seem to be aware of the existence of the

British tradition in the Marxist study of the political economy of communication, culture and the media. The works of Murdock, Golding and related scholars from this field are not mentioned once.

Raymond Williams is an exception: Sum and Jessop discuss some of his works. Williams' Cultural Materialism is situated on the border between Marxist cultural studies that originated in the humanities and Marxist media and communication studies that has traditionally been more situated in the social sciences. It is, however, obvious that Jessop and Sum have read Williams only superficially. They argue, for example, that Williams 'placed culture "inside" the economic base and, indeed, whether Williams recognized it or not, marked a return to the Marx and Engels of *The German Ideology*' (Sum & Jessop 2013: 117). One gets the impression that Sum and Jessop assume that Williams has an interesting approach, but did not engage enough with Marx's works. Such an assumption is, however, based on a reading of Williams that is not thorough enough. Works such as *Marxism and Literature* (Williams 1977) and *Marx on Culture* (Williams 1989: 195–225) are among the most thorough discussions of Marx's ideas on culture, including *The German Ideology*. These works show that Williams was not only a thorough reader of Marx, but that he profoundly engaged with the meanings of Marx's works sentence-by-sentence. Williams discusses in detail the specific meanings terms such as ideology and culture take on in Marx's writings. Sum and Jessop mention neither of these two works. They also overlook (Sum & Jessop 2013: 120, table 3.1) that Williams did not just use Gramsci for introducing the notion of the structures of feeling, but that he also used Gramsci's concept of hegemony for conceptualising culture's role in society (Williams 1977: 108–14).

The title *Towards a Cultural Political Economy* implies that such an approach has not yet been established, which only makes things worse: Decades of Marxist scholarship in the political economy of communication and culture are indirectly declared as being non-existent. One wonders how such a lack of engagement is possible. The only answer is that Sum and Jessop do not take media and communication studies seriously. And this circumstance is a more general pattern within Marxist theory. The media, communication and cultural studies fields are often seen as being soft, superstructural, secondary and not real parts of Marxist theory. This is one of the reasons why we need a media and communications-oriented companion to Marx's *Capital Volume 1*. Such a book wants to suggest to people interested in Marx that communication and communications matter for understanding capitalism just like capitalism matters for understanding communication(s).

2.5 THE POLITICAL ECONOMY AND CRITICAL THEORY OF THE INTERNET AND DIGITAL MEDIA

Since the rise of the World Wide Web (WWW) in the mid-1990s, Internet studies has become a distinct interdisciplinary field (Consalvo & Ess 2012) that analyses the mutual shaping of the Internet, on the one hand, and humans in society, on the other hand. Internet studies is overall a fairly positivist and administrative field of research. There has, however, especially in the past 15 years been an increasing number of critical and Marxist theorists and researchers who have engaged in analysing digital media and the Internet's role in capitalist society.

In 1999, Nick Dyer-Witheford published the book *Cyber-Marx*, in which he shows the importance of Marx's theory for critically understanding the Internet's contradictions in capitalism and struggles in the digital age. Dyer-Witheford (1999: 2) proposes a 'Marxism for the Marx of the Difference Engine'. Digital media are in digital capitalism highly contradictory. For understanding the complex relations of the old and the new, opportunities and risks, continuities and discontinuities, agency and structures, production and consumption, the private and the public, labour and play, leisure-time and labour-time, the commodity and the commons, etc. in the age of the Internet, Marx's dialectical theory is well suited as the foundation. It may therefore be no coincidence that Marx has been an important reference in theories of the Internet. In his works, Marx elaborated a dialectical analysis of technology in capitalism, analysed the new media of his time (such as the telegraph), pointed out the importance of the means of communication in the organisation, acceleration and globalisation of capitalism, discussed the freedom of the press and its limits in a capitalist society, anticipated the emergence of an information economy and society in his analysis of the general intellect, and was himself a practising investigative journalist, whose sharp criticisms and polemics can still inspire critical writings today. Marx was himself not just a critic of capitalism, but also a critical sociologist of the media and communications, which is another reason why critical theorists of the Internet have found interest in his works.

In his work the *Grundrisse*, Marx (1857/58: 161) described a global information network in which 'everyone attempts to inform himself' about others and 'connections are introduced'. Such a description not only sounds like an anticipation of the concept of the Internet, it is also an indication that Marx's thought is relevant for media/communication studies and the study of the Internet and social media. This passage in the *Grundrisse* is an indication that although the Internet as technology was a product of the Cold War and Californian counter-culture, Marx already anticipated its concept in the nineteenth century: *Karl Marx invented the Internet!*

When Vincent Mosco and I put together a call for a special issue of the journal *tripleC: Communication, Capitalism & Critique* with the title 'Marx is Back: The Importance of Marxist Theory and Research for Critical Communication Studies Today', we not only received a large number of submissions of abstracts, but a share of them focused on Marxist studies of the Internet and digital media. The issue was published in 2012 (Fuchs & Mosco 2012). In 2016, we published a revised version of the special issue contributions combined with additional articles as two books with a total of 1,200 pages: *Marx and the Political Economy of the Media* (Fuchs & Mosco 2016a) and *Marx in the Age of Digital Capitalism* (Fuchs & Mosco 2016b). Sixteen of the 34 chapters focus on the Marxist analysis of digital media. They make up the entire second volume, which is an indication that digital media is a predominant topic in the Marxist analysis of media and communication.

Important topics in the Marxist analysis of digital media and the Internet include (see Fuchs 2012 for a detailed discussion): (1) the dialectics of the Internet; (2) digital capitalism; (3) commodification and digital media's commodity forms; (4) labour, surplus-value, exploitation, alienation and class in the digital age; (5) globalisation and the Internet; (6) ideologies of and on the Internet; (7) digital class struggles; (8) the digital commons; (9) the digital public sphere; (10) digital media and communism; and (11) digital media aesthetics. Book-length example studies in digital Marxism include analyses of online surveillance (Andrejevic 2007), the history of the computer and the Internet (Barbrook 2007), Internet ideologies (Dean 2010; Fisher 2010; Mosco 2004), computer games (Dyer-Witheford & De Peuter 2009), the cybertariat (Huws 2003), digital capitalism (Schiller 2000), hacking culture (Söderberg 2008; Wark 2004), social media (Fuchs 2015b, 2017c), digital labour (Dyer-Witheford 2015; Fuchs 2014a; Huws 2015), cloud computing (Mosco 2014), digital peer production (Moore & Karatzogianni 2009), etc.

A range of Marxist theory approaches has been used for studying digital media, including autonomist Marxism, British cultural studies, Marxist crisis theories, cultural materialism, the Frankfurt School, Gramsci's philosophy of praxis, humanist Marxism, labour-process theory, Freudian Marxism, Hegelian Marxism, labour theory of value, Marxist feminism, Marxist geography, monopoly capitalism theory, post-colonialist theory, post-Marxism, Smythe's theory of audience labour, Situationism, structural Marxism, theories of imperialism and new imperialism, etc. The point is that there is not one best-suited interpretation and reading of Marx for critically understanding the Internet and digital media. One should rather in an open approach cherish the diversity of digital and communications-Marxism and foster solidarity and mutual aid between its representatives because being a Marxist scholar often means having to face various forms of repression (Lent & Amazeen 2015).

The Marxist study of the Internet and communication is certainly a vivid field that is, however, often not taken seriously enough in Marxist theory and politics at large. Media, communication, culture and the digital are therefore at best side notes or completely ignored in the majority of Marxist publications. I will next discuss two prominent examples.

2.6 READING MARX WITH DAVID HARVEY AND MICHAEL HEINRICH

Marx (1867: 89) acknowledged the difficulties reading *Capital* may provide: 'Beginnings are always difficult in all sciences. The understanding of the first chapter, especially the section that contains the analysis of commodities, will therefore present the greatest difficulty.' It is easier to read and discuss *Capital* in a group and to use a companion that guides the reading. Companions to Marx's *Capital* serve a quite practical purpose. They are intended to be read together and to support the critical understanding of capitalism that Marx develops step-by-step.

Two recent guides to Marx's *Capital* are David Harvey's (2010, 2013) *A Companion to Marx's Capital* and the English translation of Michael Heinrich's (2012) *An Introduction to the Three Volume of Karl Marx's Capital* that was first published in German in 2004. Heinrich's book is a short introduction consisting of 12 chapters that focus on key categories such as capitalism, critique of political economy, value/labour/money, capital/surplus-value/exploitation, profit, crisis, communism, etc. The problem with this structure is that most readers engage with Marx's *Capital* in a sequential way, reading it chapter-by-chapter. A companion is therefore only helpful if it is written as a chapter-by-chapter reading guide.

Harvey in contrast to Heinrich partly discusses *Capital* chapter-by-chapter. There are, however, some unnecessary diversions from this approach: He discusses *Volume 1*'s chapters 8 and 9 in one section, which makes it impossible to see which categories and discussions belong to which of the two chapters. He does the same for chapters 19–22. He also skips over chapters 17 and 18 with the remark that they 'do not pose any substantial issues' (Harvey 2010: 240). What Harvey actually means is that for his particular interpretation of Marxist theory, these chapters do not pose substantial issues. In my own reading guide to *Capital Volume 1*, I point out that these chapters are helpful for illustrating how to think about the rate of profit, the rate of surplus-value, paid and unpaid labour in the information industries.

Different readings of *Capital* have different priorities, which arise from the fact that Marxist theory is a broad approach uniting different schools and traditions that foreground different aspects of the critique of capitalism and class. Harvey summarises chapters 26–33 as part of one chapter. This move is certainly appropriate because in the German edition, Marx treats chapters 26–32 as one long chapter on primitive accumulation that has seven sections. In his *A Companion to Marx's Capital Volume 2*, Harvey summarises the chapters of *Capital Volumes 2 & 3* in 11 chapters.

Both Harvey's and Heinrich's books are particular interpretations of Marx's *Capital*. Harvey's lifetime achievement is that he has opened up Marxist theory to the engagement with issues of geography. Space, the global, land and the urban have today become major topics in Marxist theorising thanks to Harvey and others. Harvey has created a sensitivity that for a Marxist understanding of capitalism and society, not just issues related to time, such as labour-time and the labour theory of value, but also space and geography are of fundamental importance. Space and time are dialectically connected. Harvey's companion to *Volume 1* relatively frequently discusses aspects of geography and space, which reflects his own position as a Marxist geographer. Space is an important category for a critical theory of capitalism. But so are communication and communication technologies (what Marx terms the means of communication).

2.7 COMMUNICATION(S) IN DAVID HARVEY'S WORKS
AND HIS COMPANION TO MARX'S *CAPITAL*

Harvey has always given attention to the role of technology in capitalism. In *The Limits to Capital*, originally published in 1982, chapter 8 bears the title 'Fixed Capital' (Harvey 1982/2006: 204–38). Chapter 4 focuses on 'Technological Change, the Labour Process and the Value Composition of Capital' (Harvey 1982/2006: 98–136).

> Marx's analysis of the contradictory 'laws of motion' of capitalism rests heavily upon understanding the swift-flowing currents and deep perturbations associated with technological change. Although Marx's conception of technology is very broad, he accords a certain priority to the instruments of labour – machinery in particular – as major weapons in the fight to preserve the accumulation of capital. Such instruments of labour can be used in the competitive struggle for relative surplus value, to increase the physical and value productivity of labour power and to reduce the demand for labour (thereby pushing wage rates down via the formation of an industrial reserve army). They can also be used to bring the power of past 'dead' labour to bear over living labour in the work process, with all manner of consequences for the labourer ... . These are awesome weapons that the capitalists can command once the latter have assumed control over the means of production. (Harvey 1982/2006: 204)

In *A Companion to Marx's Capital*, Harvey devotes chapters 7 and 8 and a total of 46 pages to *Capital Volume 1*'s chapter 15, the technology chapter 'Machinery and Large-Scale Industry' (Harvey 2010a: 189–235). Harvey's conclusion to *Capital Volume 1*'s chapter 15 is that Marx

> plainly believes that the application of science and technology can have progressive implications. But the big problem in this chapter is to figure out where, exactly, these progressive possibilities might lie and how they can be mobilized in the quest to create a socialist mode of production. ... Technological and organizational changes are not a *deus ex machine*, but deeply embedded in the coevolution of our relation to nature, processes of production, social relations, mental concepts of the world and the reproduction of daily life. (Harvey 2010a: 234–5)

That technology relates to mental concepts means, on the one hand, that in capitalism it often takes on the ideological form of a technological fetish as in technological determinism. But mental aspects of technology also refer to the fact that information and communication technologies are means for distributing data and knowledge over spatio-temporal distances and thereby help in organising social relations (including capital relations and capital-labour relations). Harvey has again and again given attention to communication technologies as attributes of space.

So, for example, in *The Limits to Capital*, he writes that 'transport and communications systems, stretched in far-flung nets around the globe, permit information and ideas as well as material goods and even labour power to move around with relative ease' (Harvey 1982/2006: 373). Harvey's concept of time-space-compression lies at the intersection of the concept of space and the concepts of the means of communication and the means of transport:

[There is a] history of successive waves of time-space compression generated out of the pressures of capital accumulation with its perpetual search to annihilate space through time and reduce turnover time. (Harvey 1989: 306–7)

The rise of capitalism's flexible accumulation regime since the mid-1970s has entailed

a new round of what I shall call 'time-space compression' … in the capitalist world – the time horizons of both private and public decision-making have shrunk, while satellite communication and declining transport costs have made it increasingly possible to spread those decisions immediately over an ever wider and variegated space. (Harvey 1989: 147)

Capital accumulation has always been about speed-up (consider the history of technological innovations in production processes, marketing, money exchanges) and revolutions in transport and communications (the railroad and telegraph, radio and automobile, jet transport and telecommunications), which have the effect of reducing spatial barriers. The experience of time and space has periodically been radically transformed. We see a particularly strong example of this kind of radical transformation since around 1970: the impact of telecommunications, jet cargo transport, containerization of road, rail and ocean transport, the development of futures markets, electronic banking and computerized production systems. We have recently been going through a strong phase of what I call 'time-space compression': the world suddenly feels much smaller, and the time-horizons over which we can think about social action become much shorter. (Harvey 2001: 123)

More recently, Harvey has also in single passages commented on the role of social media and digital labour in contemporary capitalism: 'capital mobilises consumers to produce their own spectacle via YouTube, Facebook, Twitter and other forms of social media' (Harvey 2014: 236). 'It is also interesting that some of the most vigorous sectors of development in our times – like Google and Facebook and the rest of the digital labour sector – have grown very fast on the back of free labour' (Harvey 2017: 102).

What was initially conceived as a liberatory regime of collaborative production of an open access commons has been transformed into a regime of hyper-exploitation upon which capital freely feeds. The unrestrained pillage by big capital (like Amazon and Google) of the free goods produced by a self-skilled labour force has become a major feature of our times. (Harvey 2017: 96)

Harvey leaves the exact economic processes of how social media corporations use targeted advertising as a capital accumulation model open. But one must take into consideration that he works on a general theory of capitalism. It should certainly be seen positively that he recognises the relevance of capitalism's digital dimension. Harvey stresses that cognitive capitalism is not a radically new phase of capitalism or society, but requires older forms of labour, such as assemblage labour (for a detailed analysis of the international division of digital labour, see Fuchs 2014a, 2016b):

Hence the claim that we are entering a new phase of capitalism in which knowledge is pre-eminent and that a brilliant techno-utopia based on that knowledge and all its labour-saving innovations (such as automation and artificial intelligence) is just around the corner or, as someone like Paul Mason maintains, already here. Such a redefinition may look about right from the perspective of Silicon Valley, but it falls on its face in the collapsing factories of Bangladesh and the suicide-ridden employment zones of both industrial Shenzhen and rural India where microfinance has spread its net to foster the mother of all sub-prime lending crises. (Harvey 2017: 104)

Countering the techno-determinist and techno-optimist assumption that the rebellions and revolutions of the Arab Spring were Facebook revolutions and Twitter revolts, David Harvey comments that the Arab Spring and the Occupy movement show that 'it is bodies on the street and in the squares, not the babble of sentiments on Twitter or Facebook, that really matter' (Harvey 2012: 162). Empirical studies (Fuchs 2014b) have shown that both techno-determinist and techno-ignorant accounts of the role of social media in social struggles are one-dimensional: It is not true that activists in occupations tend to either communicate face-to-face or via social media. They do both. There is no binary between online and offline protest communication. And even more than this, there tends to be a reinforcing dialectic of face-to-face and social media communication: The more active protestors are in occupations and demonstrations, the larger their social network among activists tends to be, the more they engage face-to-face with other activists, which is also an incentive to take protest communication, organisation and mobilisation to social media. Occupied squares are social spaces that are constructed, reproduced, developed and defended in and through communicative social relations that take place offline and online and as dialectical entanglement of both. There is a complex dialectic of communication and society.

In one passage in *A Companion to Marx's Capital*, David Harvey asks, 'do you really need a mobile phone nowadays?' (Harvey 2010a: 106). The answer for around 5 billion people in the world is: Yes, definitely! The point is not to challenge the mobile phone as such, but the capitalist organisation of mobility that makes people conduct productive labour nearly anytime from everywhere and collapses the boundaries between leisure and labour as well as the exploitative production conditions of mobile phones in capitalism's international division of labour. The convergence of work and free time is not automatically a problem in itself if it means that work becomes more playful, social and self-determined. The problem under neoliberalism and capitalism is, however, that productive labour tends to enter and soak up leisure-time, resulting in absolute surplus-value production, not the other way around.

When David Harvey discusses means of communication in Marx's works in general terms, he tends to see them as attributes of space, which is a logical consequence of his stress on the need of space and the 'geographical revolution' he has brought about in Marxist theory. For example, Harvey comments on Marx's remark that the 'transformation of the mode of production in one sphere of industry necessitates a similar transformation in other spheres' (Marx 1867: 505). Harvey remarks that this passage 'introduces one of the other themes that I find extremely interesting in Marx: that is the importance of what he calls in the *Grundrisse* the "annihilation of space by time"' (Harvey 2010a: 206). This interest has in Harvey's own work been reflected in the discussion of information and communication technologies as means of time-space-compression (Harvey 1989).

Information and communication technologies, including the computer, certainly play a key role in accelerating the circulation of commodities in space-time. This is not their only role. Media also communicate ideologies, such as political ideologies and commodity ideology in the form of commercial advertisements. Computers and computer networks are not only organisers of the circulation of commodities, but also the means of production for the creation of information products. They are furthermore the platforms for companies' internal and external communication. While trains, buses, automobiles, ships, lorries and airplanes transport people and physical goods, computer networks transport information, information products and flows of communication. The computer is a universal machine that is simultaneously a means of production, circulation and consumption.

Overall, it is evident that Harvey has interest in issues of technology, communication(s) and the digital and therefore again and again mentions these issues. His approach can certainly act as one of the foundations of a Marxist theory of communication, but is itself not such an approach because its main focus is on the question of capitalism's spatial relations. One possibility for going with Harvey beyond Harvey is to think of how space relates to communication (see Fuchs 2019).

Communication is not only an attribute of space-time. Social relations create, reproduce and organise social spaces, which means that human communication produces and reproduces social space and social space conditions, that is, enables and constrains communication through which social space is further reproduced, created, etc. For Harvey, communication is an attribute of space. But there is a dialectic of social space and communication.

Humans produce social relations that are bounded, related and organised in social spaces. In the production of social relations, they produce and reproduce social structures that enable and constrain the practices in social systems. Specific social systems form society's key institutions. Humans produce and reproduce social relations, social structures, social systems, institutions and social spaces that in a dialectical manner condition (enable and constrain) human practices and are the medium and outcome of such practices. Communication is the process in which structures, social systems, institutions and social spaces are lived and thereby reproduced by humans in a concrete manner in everyday life. They do so by making use of particular communicative means of production (verbal and non-verbal codes/languages, information and communication technologies) that enable the production and reproduction of the social: Humans produce social relations by making meaning of each other and thereby reproduce the structures, systems, institutions and spaces that enable and constrain their communication. Communication is the way in which humans live and produce social relations that, in turn, constitute structures, systems, institutions and spaces. Communication is the everyday process that establishes and maintains social relations. It is the production and reproduction of social relations. Humans (re)produce social structures through communication in their everyday lives and thereby (re)produce societal structures that frame, condition, enable and constrain communicative production in everyday life.

2.8 COMMUNICATION(S) IN MICHAEL HEINRICH'S INTRODUCTION TO *CAPITAL*

Michael Heinrich argues in his companion that his book 'stands within the substantive context of this "new reading of Marx"' (Heinrich 2012: 27) established by the works of Hans-Georg Backhaus and Helmut Reichelt. 'The differences between this new reading and traditional Marxist political economy will become clearer throughout the course of this work' (Heinrich 2012: 27). Heinrich did not intend to write an introduction that helps reading Marx from a specific topical perspective, such as communication or space, but one that uses a particular approach, the

New Reading of Marx school of thought. 'My presentation thus builds on a particular interpretation of Marx's theory, while others are dismissed' (Heinrich 2012: 10).

Heinrich in this introductory book to Marx's three volumes of *Capital* claims that 'Marx's value theory is rather a monetary theory of value' (Heinrich 2012: 63). This assumption is a particular and certainly not a universally valid interpretation of Marx's value concept. It argues for a monetary theory of value, whereas another possible interpretation is to set out a value theory and critique of money that is grounded in the labour theory of value. The problem is that Heinrich's book may deceive readers and create the impression that a specific interpretation of Marx – the one advanced by Backhaus, Reichelt, Heinrich and their colleagues – is Marx's original and own version of the labour theory of value.

Heinrich argues that 'value also first exists in exchange' and that the 'substance of value' is 'not inherent to individual commodities, but is bestowed *mutually* in the act of exchange' (Heinrich 2012: 53). The problem that I see is that Heinrich's approach implies that no exploitation has taken place if a commodity is not sold. Let us assume that a company employs 100 employees, who work 16,000 hours per month and produce during this time 16,000 television sets as well as a marketing and branding strategy and campaign. They are not doing well in competition because the average industry standard is a production of 16,000 sets in 8,000 hours. Therefore, the company does not sell a single television and the workers do not get paid. They, however, still produce television sets. According to Heinrich, all of these workers are not exploited and the TV sets do not contain value because they are not sold and so not transformed into the money form. An alternative interpretation is to distinguish between two forms of value as average labour-time and monetary value. In the example, the average labour-time that is socially necessary in the television industry to produce one TV set is 30 minutes. A TV's average value at the company level is 1 hour, which constitutes competitive disadvantages in the realisation of monetary value. No matter if the manufacturing and advertising workers in the example get paid or not and no matter if the commodities they produce are sold or not, their labour has produced commodities that objectify their labour-time and that they do not own. They are therefore productive and exploited workers. Heinrich's understanding of value underestimates the difficulty of conceptualising productive labour, class and exploitation.

Marx's *Fragment on Machines* in the *Grundrisse* has in the past years especially in autonomist Marxism resulted in discussions about information work and technology. Heinrich (2014) is sceptical about the *Fragment* and argues about a formulation of the general intellect: 'With that, production based on exchange value breaks down, and the direct, material production process is stripped of the form of penury and antithesis' (Marx 1857/58: 705). This formulation has again and again resulted in controversies. Heinrich (2014: 197) interprets it as meaning that Marx in the *Grundrisse* had a 'one-sided conception of crisis' (Heinrich 2014: 197) and predicted that the employment of machinery in capitalism 'should have the consequence that capitalist production … collapses' (Heinrich 2014: 207). But one must see that with the formulation 'With that' Marx means in reference back to the preceding sentence a condition where the 'surplus labour of the mass has ceased to be the condition for the development of general wealth' (Marx 1857/58: 705). So when he speaks of a breakdown in the *Fragment*, Marx does not mean an automatic collapse of capitalism, but rather that exchange-value collapses within communism and that the rise of knowledge work and automation bring about a fundamental antagonism of necessary labour-time and surplus labour-time. The establishment of communism, however, presupposes a conscious revolutionary sublation of capitalism. The *Fragment* does not formulate an automatic breakdown of capitalism.

Heinrich not only dismisses the *Fragment* and its relevance for understanding the information economy today. In his introduction to *Capital*, he mentions means of communication only once very briefly (Heinrich 2012: 206), the Internet one time in a footnote (Heinrich 2012: 237, footnote 68), the mobile phone and the WWW never. Heinrich does not seem to consider information, communication and culture as important dimensions for a Marxian critique of the political economy.

There has also been a controversial discussion of Heinrich's approach in respect to crisis theory and the law of the tendency of the profit rate to fall. Heinrich (2013) argues that this law is flawed and that Marxist theory needs to explain crises without it. 'In contrast to Marx, we cannot assume a "law of the tendency of the rate of profit to fall"' (Heinrich 2013: 153). Others argue against Heinrich that such a law is consistent on Marx's own terms, is crucial for understanding the capitalist economy's contradictions, and that Heinrich attempts to eliminate Marx's crisis theory (see, e.g., Kliman et al. 2013). No matter which position one takes in this debate, it shows that Heinrich advances a particular interpretation of Marx.

Given that diverse interpretations of Marx are possible and needed, Heinrich's particularism is unproblematic and welcome. The problem is, however, the aura of universality that his book evokes by using the title *An Introduction to the Three Volumes of Karl Marx's Capital*. A more appropriate title would be *Michael Heinrich's New Reading of Karl Marx's Three Volumes of Capital*. My own guide to *Capital Volume 1* (Fuchs 2016d) does not claim to be a universal or the only valid interpretation and does not use a particular school of Marxist thought such as Marxist spatial theory or the New Reading of Marx School. It rather sets out to help the reader use Marx's categories as tools of thought for critically understanding media, communication, culture, technology and the Internet today. The title *Reading Marx in the Information Age: A Media and Communication Studies Perspective on Capital Volume 1* sets out in contrast to Harvey and Heinrich that the book does not want to be a general introduction, but one that is concretely mediated with one of the important contemporary political-economic challenges, namely, the media and communication system's role in capitalism. It foregrounds the importance of a specific topic, not particular schools or approaches. Marx's own thought was historical and dialectical, which means that reading Marx today should best be done in a historically specific way, relating it to twenty-first-century capitalism, which requires us to think about how to dialectically update Marx's categories based on a dialectic of continuity and emergent properties. Digital media did not exist at the time of Marx, but nonetheless his works are a powerful foundation for understanding the role of the computer and communication(s) in capitalism today.

2.9 IN WHAT RESPECT DOES MARX MATTER FOR UNDERSTANDING COMMUNICATION(S)?

Marx was not just a critical theorist, but also a critical journalist, politician and polemicist. His interventionist and critical style of argumentation is something that today is often missing in the news media and can therefore serve as a good example for critical writing. Marx was a dialectical thinker. Dialectics as an instrument of complex thinking allows us to understand the contradictions of the media in capitalism. Think, for example, of the contradiction between users who like to download digital content without payment online, and media corporations that use intellectual property rights, policing, censorship and surveillance for trying to limit online file sharing. Profits and wages are, however, dialectically mediated in capitalism, which adds another contradiction so that also some artists perceive file sharing as a threat. Another contradiction in the culture industry is one between the two class factions of the content industry and the openness industry: The first commodifies content, the second lives from open content on the Internet that it combines with other accumulation strategies, such as targeted advertising. The likes of YouTube and Facebook do not necessarily oppose file sharing of copyrighted content because openness benefits their businesses. Openness in this context means the availability of digital content online without payment. The openness industry uses other ways to accumulate capital, especially advertising. The contradiction between the openness industry and the content industry shows that the online economy is dialectical: It is full of contradictions.

The commodity is capitalism's 'elementary form' (Marx 1867: 125). Marx's commodity analysis and critique allows us to understand the media's forms of commodification. Information is a peculiar commodity: It is not used up in consumption, can easily and quickly be copied and distributed, has high initial production costs and low copy costs, involves high risks and uncertainty about whether it is saleable or not, is non-rivalrous in consumption and requires special protective measures to be turned into a scarce good from whose consumption others can be excluded. Capital accumulation in the information economy therefore requires special strategies, such as the commodification of content along with intellectual property rights and copyrights, the commodification of access to content (e.g. subscriptions), the commodification of production, distribution and consumption technologies, the commodification of audiences in advertising, the multiplication of media formats and the re-use of content, or the commodification of users and the data they generate in targeted online advertising.

Class is a key category in Marx's analysis. It is related to concepts such as exploitation, surplus-value, the working class/proletariat and productive labour. The 'proletarian is merely a machine for the production of surplus-value, the capitalist too is merely a machine for the transformation of this surplus-value into surplus capital' (Marx 1867: 742). In the age of the Internet and the culture industry, class is still a crucial category, but has become more variegated. We have to consider the class status and interests of unpaid interns, online freelancers, unremunerated users of Facebook and Google who create economic value, different forms of knowledge workers, a new young precariat that is attracted to work in the culture industry, Foxconn workers in China who assemble mobile phones and laptops, miners in Africa who extract minerals that form the physical foundation of digital media technologies and who work under slave-like conditions, software engineers who are highly paid and work very long overtime hours, etc. There is what can be called an international division of digital labour (Fuchs 2014a, 2015b: chapter 6).

Ideology naturalises domination and exploitation. Such naturalisation is according to Marx immanent to the commodity form itself as commodity fetishism. Media are key tools for the production, dissemination and consumption of political and corporate ideologies. The 'definite social relation between men themselves' assumes 'the fantastic form of a relation between things' (Marx 1867: 165). Advertising makes use of the void that commodity fetishism leaves by rendering the social relations of production invisible in the commodity itself. Advertising fills this void by product propaganda. If you think of Facebook, then the commodity status is not immediately visible because you do not pay for access: Your immediate experience is the sociality you enjoy on the platform with others. The social veils Facebook's commodity form. Commodity fetishism takes on an inverted form on Facebook (Fuchs 2014a: chapter 11): In regular commodity fetishism, things (commodities, money) veil social relations. On corporate social media, social relations are the immediate and concrete experience, whereas the commodity form only indirectly confronts the users. The social character of these platforms veils the commodity form of these platforms. Facebook and Google do not sell access or communication, but are the world's largest advertising companies.

Marx stresses that communication technologies are the medium and outcome of economic and societal globalisation. There is a dialectic of globalisation and communication. Marx also develops a dialectical understanding of technology in *Capital* and the *Grundrisse*. He analysed the contradictions of technology in capitalism. From Marx's analysis of technology we can learn that communication and other technologies are not evil or good as such, but that their effects depend on how they are constructed, designed and used within society. At the same time, technologies can have unpredictable consequences, especially if they are highly complex systems. Marx anticipated the emergence of an information economy by arguing that with the development of the productive forces, the role of knowledge, technology and science in production increases. His notion of the general intellect is of particular importance in this context. He argued that technology also socialises labour, which comes into a contradiction with class relations. Today we can observe this contradiction in a new form, as antagonism between the digital, networked productive forces and class relations. An example is that digitisation can turn knowledge into a gift that is distributed online. But in a capitalist society, people depend on wages for survival so that the online gift economy under capitalist class relations does not bring about a democratic communism, but rather poses mere alternative potentials. It enforces the precarisation of digital and cultural labour in capitalism. It is a contested question in the Left how to react to this contradiction. Some see the Internet as an enemy they oppose, others celebrate it as taking communism online as digital gift economy. A more nuanced assessment is that there are potentials to turn knowledge into a digital commons, but that within capitalism it is also important that cultural producers can survive based on a wage, which opens up new ideas, for example, the need for introducing a universal basic income or a participatory media fee that is funded by corporate taxation and that via participatory budgeting allows citizens to donate to non-commercial media companies.

Capitalism's contradictions again and again result in crises. The Internet economy has, for example, been hit by a deep crisis in 2000, the so-called dot-com crisis, in which many Internet companies went bankrupt. It was already back then highly financialised. Financialisation is another concept that Marx discusses in detail, especially in *Capital Volume 3*, where he introduces the concept of fictitious capital. He also stresses that capitalism has an inherent concentration and monopoly tendency. Information industries are highly prone to concentration because of mechanisms such as the advertising-circulation-spiral: Media with a large number of readers, viewers, listeners and users tend to attract more advertising revenues, which allows them competitive advantages that can result in a further expansion of their audiences and more market concentration. In the media world, concentration not only has to do with economic power, but due to the nature of information also with ideological power, the concentration of the power to disseminate ideas.

Marx foregrounded the importance of social struggles for a just and fair society, that is, a participatory democracy. As long as class societies exist, class struggles remain a reality. Activists communicate among themselves and to the public. Communication technologies, such as social media, the mobile phone or e-mail, are therefore key organisation tools in social movements and political parties. Marx allows us to better understand the nature of social struggles in modern society. Last, but not least, Marx had a vision of an alternative to capitalism. It often seems today that the Internet or the media are best organised as corporations. There are, however, also alternative traditions. Think of public service broadcasters that do not use advertising, knowledge as commons on Wikipedia, the free software movement, free public WiFi initiatives, not-for-profit online sharing platforms such as Freecycle or Streetbank.

Marx's idea of communism reminds us that the commodity form is inappropriate for basic human aspects of society such as love, education, knowledge and communication. If the commodity form implies inequality, then a truly fair, democratic and just society must be a commons-based society. For the communication system, this means that communication systems as commons correspond to the essence of humanity, society and democracy. Commons such as knowledge are not produced by single individuals, but have a social, historical and co-operative character. They are produced by universal work: 'Universal labour is all scientific work, all discovery and invention. It is brought about partly by the cooperation of men now living, but partly also by building on earlier work' (Marx 1894: 199). Whenever new information emerges, it incorporates the whole societal history of information, that is, information has a historical character. Hence, it seems to be self-evident that information should be a common good, freely available to all. But in global informational capitalism, information has become an important productive force that favours new forms of capital accumulation. Information is today often not treated as a public good and common, but rather as a commodity. There is an antagonism between information as a common good and as a commodity.

2.10 FOR A COMMUNICATION REVOLUTION IN MARXIST THEORY!

Marxist theory too often treats communication as a superstructure. Such analyses are contradicted by the fact that knowledge and communication have not only become important commodities, but are also shaped by a twenty-first-century antagonism between the communication commons and communication commodities. The time has come for a media and communication-oriented revolution of Marxist theory. Communication is still one of Marxism's blind spots, on which only a media and communication studies-oriented reading of *Capital* can shed light.

Marx discussed the implications of the telegraph for the globalisation of trade, production and society, was one of the first philosophers and sociologists of technology in modern society, anticipated the role of knowledge labour and the rise of an information society and was himself a critical journalist. This shows that somebody who cares about the analysis of media and communication has many reasons to engage with Marx. He stressed the importance of the concept of the social: He highlighted that phenomena in society (such as money or markets and, today, the Internet, Facebook, Twitter, etc.) do not simply exist, but are the outcome of social relations between human beings. They do not exist automatically and by necessity because humans can change society. Therefore, society and the media are open for change and contain the possibility of a better future. If we want to understand what is social about social media, then reading Marx can help us a lot.

Today there is much talk about 'social media', although the likes of Facebook, Twitter and Google are privately owned corporations listed on the stock market and therefore expressions of possessive individualism (Fuchs 2017c). Marx reminds us that capitalism is incompletely social. True social media can only exist in a commons-based participatory democracy. Marx's works are key intellectual tools for the inspiration of struggles for a commons-based society and commons-based media.

3

Rereading Marx as Critical Sociologist of Technology

3.1 INTRODUCTION

The task of this chapter is to reread Marx's concept and critical sociology of technology by tracing the development of his notion of machinery and the role of technology in capitalism in his works from the 1840s up until the publication of *Capital Volume 1* in 1867.

Karl Marx saw technology as an important feature of capitalist society. His analysis of technology, or what he also refers to as means of production, fixed constant capital and machinery, is dialectical in several respects:

1. By analysing technology based on a dialectic of technology and society, Marx avoids both technological determinism and social construction of technology.
2. Marx is neither a techno-optimist nor a techno-pessimist, but stresses that technology in an antagonistic society has antagonistic effects: There is in most cases not just one impact of technology on society, but several ones that contradict each other.
3. Marx analyses technology based on a dialectic of exploitation and liberation: In capitalism, technology is a means of relative surplus-value production and control. At the same time, it advances the contradiction between the productive forces and the relations of production so that germ forms of a commons-based society emerge that cannot be realised within capitalism and within private property relations form one of the factors contributing to economic crises. As a consequence, liberation from capital requires both the fundamental transformation of society and the re-design of technology.

These three points have been formulated most visibly in *Capital Volume 1*'s chapter 15 'Machinery and Large-Scale Industry' (for a detailed discussion, see Fuchs 2016d: chapter 15) as well as in the *Grundrisse*'s *Fragment on Machines* (for a detailed discussion, see Fuchs 2016d: appendix 2). We can therefore briefly compare these two pieces before tracing the origins of Marx's concept of technology.

3.2 *CAPITAL VOLUME I*'S CHAPTER 15 AND THE *GRUNDRISSE*'S *FRAGMENT ON MACHINES*

'Machinery and Large-Scale Industry' is with 147 printed pages out of a total of 995 pages (in the Penguin edition, including the appendix 'Results of the Immediate Process of Production') the longest chapter in *Capital Volume I* (Marx 1867: 492–639). It comprises 15 per cent of the total length of the first volume of Marx's main work. The chapter consists of ten sections that focus on the development of machinery (15.1), machinery and value (15.2), machinery's impacts on labour in capitalism (15.3), the machine and the factory (15.4), machinery and class struggle (15.5), the question labour replaced by machinery can be compensated by new jobs created by the use of new technology (15.6), machinery and the attraction and repulsion of labour (15.7), modern industry's transformation of earlier forms of labour (15.8), technology and legislation (15.9), and modern industry's transformation of agriculture (15.10).

Chapter 15 grounds a critical theory of technology by analysing technology's role in capitalism as contradictory means of production that acts as means of relative surplus-value production and control and ripens the antagonism between the productive forces and the relations of production. The chapter shows that Marx's theory is not abstract, but grounded in an analysis of empirical reality. Marx quotes from and analyses factory inspectors' reports in order to ground his theoretical categories in workers' everyday reality. Furthermore, concreteness is achieved by relating modern technology to working class struggles for the reduction of the working day and aspects of labour legislation. One can learn from chapter 15 that technology's effects on society are not pre-given, but are subject to class struggles.

Marx starts the analysis in chapter 15 at the abstract level by defining machinery as the unit of the motor mechanism, the transmitting mechanism and the tool or working machine (Marx 1867: 494). But the abstract is at the same time concrete: Marx already in the chapter's first paragraph of the first section makes clear that machinery's essence has developed historically together with capitalism so that 'machinery is intended to cheapen commodities' and 'is a means for producing surplus-value' (Marx 1867: 492). By a dialectical method of theory and empirical inquiry Marx in chapter 15 works out modern technology's antagonistic character: He shows that the means of production does not just produce a dialectic of the production of capital and the production of communist potentials, but that this dialectic is mediated through a negative dialectic, in which technology acts as a means of destruction that advances capitalism's antagonisms, including exploitation, unemployment, precarious labour and crisis potentials. Marx therefore ends chapter 15 by stressing modern technology's role in the 'process of destruction' that results in 'simultaneously undermining the original sources of all wealth – the soil and the worker' (Marx 1867: 638).

The *Fragment of Machines* is a section in the *Grundrisse's* sixth and seventh notebooks (Marx 1857/58: 690–714). Given that the *Grundrisse* was *Capital's* first draft, we can consider the *Fragment* as a draft of *Capital Volume I's* chapter 15. Pier Aldo Rovatti's 1973 article 'The Critique of Fetishism in Marx's *Grundrisse*' contains the earliest traceable use of the term 'Fragment of Machines' in English (Rovatti 1973). But the very term 'Fragment of Machines' stems from Renato Solmi's 1964 translation into Italian that was published under the title 'Frammento sulle macchine' in the journal *Quaderni Rossi*. The journal formed one of the foundations of autonomist Marxism, an interpretation of Marx that gives special attention to class struggle and the role of technology and knowledge. Consequently, the *Fragment* has played an important role in autonomist Marxism (see, e.g., Hardt & Negri 2000: section 1.2; Negri 1991: chapter 7; Vercellone 2007; Virno 1996).

In the *Fragment*, Marx introduces the notion of the general intellect (Marx 1857/58: 706), by which he anticipated the emergence of an information economy as the result of the development of the productive forces. Furthermore, he analyses the capitalist antagonism between necessary labour-time and surplus labour-time. On the one hand, Marx thereby makes clear that machinery is a factor that advances capitalist crises and working class precarity. On the other hand, he in a manner that is clearer than in other works argues that modern technology helps in creating the foundations of communism because its reduction of necessary labour-time through the increase of productivity enables a society, in which the 'measure of wealth is then not any longer, in any way, labour time, but rather disposable time' (Marx 1857/58: 708).

Roman Rosdolsky in his analysis of the *Grundrisse* highlights that Marx in the elaboration of the concept of the general intellect stresses modern technology's prospects for the working class' 'future liberation' by the 'radical reduction of working time', a development that, however, can naturally 'only be realised in a communist society; but capital – against its will – presses forward in this direction!' (Rosdolsky 1977: 243).

But under capitalist conditions, technology's productivity increases backfire and thereby deepen exploitation and advance crisis because capital 'presses to reduce labour time to a minimum, while it posits labour time, on the other side, as sole measure and source of wealth' (Marx 1857/58: 366). Modern technology's communist potentials are certainly worked out much clearer in the *Fragment* than in *Capital Volume I*'s chapter 15. So the *Fragment* goes in a certain respect beyond chapter 15. At the same time, chapter 15 is historically much more concrete and follows technology's contradictions into the experience of the working class' everyday struggles. So chapter 15 goes beyond the *Fragment* just like the *Fragment* goes beyond chapter 15.

When discussing Marx and technology, there is today much focus on chapter 15 and the *Fragment*. But Marx's analysis of machinery started earlier and is also present in other works. We will next trace the development of the categories of machinery and technology in the earlier works of Marx and Engels.

3.3 MACHINERY IN THE WORKS OF MARX AND ENGELS IN THE 1840S

In the *Economic and Philosophic Manuscripts of 1844*, Marx argues that capitalism reduces humans to the status of machines: Capital depresses the worker 'spiritually and physically to the condition of a machine' (MECW 3: 237–8). 'The machine accommodates itself to the *weakness* of the human being in order to make the *weak* human being into a machine' (MECW 3: 308). Marx here takes a humanist perspective and stresses that capitalism is inhumane and treats workers just like inanimate matter, as things and toil that can be used and abused. Capital denies workers their humanity. However, an aspect that is only briefly mentioned here and there is how the capitalist use of machines shapes working conditions. Marx: 'Since the worker has sunk to the level of a machine, he can be confronted by the machine as competitor' (MECW 3: 238).

In 1844, Engels published a series of three articles under the title 'The Condition of England'. In the second one, he argues: 'Since the application of the steam-engine and of metal cylinders in printing, one man does the work of two hundred' (MECW 3: 482). So Engels here grasps the phenomenon of technological productivity increase. But there is no special theoretical vocabulary for this phenomenon. Later, Marx introduced the notion of machine as fixed constant capital that is a tool of relative surplus-value production. In his 1845 book *The Condition of the Working-Class in England*, Engels starts the analysis with the observation that the 'history of the proletariat in England begins with the second half of the last century, with the invention of the steam-engine and of machinery for working cotton' (MECW 4: 307). Engels also describes the negative consequences of machine use under capitalist conditions: 'Every improvement in machinery throws workers out of employment' (MECW 4: 429). In *The German Ideology* (written in 1845/46), Marx and Engels argue that machinery plays a role in the international division of labour: A machine invented in England deprives 'countless workers of bread in India and China' (MECW 5: 51). A more specialised vocabulary for characterising technology's role in capitalism is still missing in these works.

In 1847, Marx published his work *The Poverty of Philosophy*, a critique of Pierre-Joseph Proudhon's 1846 book *The System of Economic Contradictions, or The Philosophy of Poverty*. The second section of Marx's book holds the title '§2: Division of Labour and Machinery' and is devoted to the analysis of technology in capitalism (MECW 6: 178–90). The underlying philosophical difference between Marx and Proudhon has to do with their interpretations of Hegel: Whereas for Proudhon, a dialectical relationship means that something has a good and a bad side so that one must preserve the first and get rid of the second, for Marx 'dialectical movement' means that two sides contradict each other, are at once different and the same, interpenetrate and overgrasp into each other, so that the solution of the contradiction is the sublation (*Aufhebung*) and negation of the negation, in which there is 'their conflict and their fusion into a new category' (MECW 6: 168).

As a consequence, the division of labour is for Proudhon an eternal feature of society that in capitalism has a good and a bad side, whereas for Marx the division of labour is an expression of class relations that need to be politically sublated through class struggles in order to humanise society. For Proudhon, 'the concentration of the instruments of labour is the negation of the division of labour' (MECW 6: 187). So Proudhon stresses only the one side of machines, whereas Marx in *The Poverty of Philosophy* stresses the dialectical character of modern machines. They simultaneously have a repressive reality and emancipatory potentials. The dialectical character of modern machines has to do with the fact that in capitalism they are embedded into the class relationship between capital and labour: 'The modern workshop, which is based on the application of machinery, is a social production relation, an economic category' (MECW 6: 183). 'In short, with the introduction of machinery the division of labour inside society has increased, the task of the worker inside the workshop has been simplified, capital has been concentrated, the human being has been further dismembered' (MECW 6: 188). The dialectical character of technology is a key feature of Marx's analysis of technology. 'Discovered' in his early philosophical works, he applied this principle in his later works to the historical and theoretical analysis of technology.

In the *Manifesto of the Communist Party*, published in February 1848, Marx and Engels stress how the capitalist application of machinery has radically transformed the production process so that large-scale industry emerged. 'Owing to the extensive use of machinery and to division of labour, the work of the proletarians has lost all individual character, and, consequently, all charm for the workman. He becomes an appendage of the machine' (MECW 6: 490–1). Marx and Engels also stress the embed-dedness of the capitalist application of technology into the antagonism of productive forces and relations of production – 'the revolt of modern productive forces against modern conditions of production' (MECW 6: 489) that creates capitalist crises. Already in *The German Ideology*, Marx and Engels spoke of the development that 'an earlier form of intercourse, which has become a fetter, is replaced by a new one corresponding to the more developed productive forces and, hence, to the advanced mode of the self-activity of individuals – a form which in its turn becomes a fetter and is then replaced by another' (MECW 5: 82). The term 'forms of intercourse' (*Verkehrsform*) was later replaced by the category of the relations of production (*Produktionsverhältnisse*).

Marx and Engels also stress that 'modern industry' creates 'improved means of communication' that 'place the workers of different localities in contact with one another (MECW 6: 493). There is a dialectic of modern communication technologies and the globalisation of production and circulation. Communication technologies shape and are shaped by transformations of society's space-time relations. Ten years later, Marx pinpointed this insight in the *Grundrisse* in the following way: 'Capital by its nature drives beyond every spatial barrier. Thus the creation of the physical conditions of exchange – of the means of communication and transport – the annihilation of space by time – becomes an extraordinary necessity for it' (Marx 1857/58: 524).

In 1849, Marx published the pamphlet *Wage Labour and Capital*. Continuing his earlier established analysis, he argues in this work that the capitalist use of machinery throws 'the hand workers onto the streets in masses' and results in the replacement of 'skilled workers by unskilled' ones (MECW 9: 226). For the first time, Marx in this essay critically questions the compensation theory of labour that says that 'the workers rendered superfluous by machinery find *new* branches of employment' (MECW 9: 226). Marx here develops a critique of the compensation theory that says that capital will do everything possible to reduce the amount of employed labour in order to maximise profit. In *Capital Volume 1*'s chapter 15 ('Machinery and Large-Scale Industry'), Marx focuses the entire subsection 15.6 on the critique of the compensation theory (Marx 1867: 565–75).

In *The German Ideology*, we find the well-known passage in which Marx defines the abolition of the division of labour and the development of well-rounded individuals as an aspect of communism: Marx speaks of a

> communist society, where nobody has one exclusive sphere of activity but each can become accomplished in any branch he wishes, society regulates the general production and thus makes it possible for me to do one thing today and another tomorrow, to hunt in the morning, fish in the afternoon, rear cattle in the evening, criticise after dinner, just as I have a mind, without ever becoming hunter, fisherman, shepherd or critic. (MECW 5: 47)

There is no reference to the role of technology in communism in this passage. Marx assumes that the antagonism of the relations of production and the productive forces creates the foundations of communism, but he only implicitly assumes without making it explicit that communism requires a high level of productivity and therefore a highly developed status of machines as its precondition in order to enable the abolishment of wage-labour and the division of labour in a post-scarcity society. As close as Marx gets to the discussion of technology in communism in *The German Ideology* is the formulation that the 'development of productive forces' is 'an absolutely necessary practical premise' and that 'communism ... presupposes the universal development of productive forces' (MECW 5: 49). Highly productive machines that reduce necessary labour-time to a minimum are not explicitly mentioned.

In the *Manifesto of the Communist Party*, Marx and Engels point out that communism is a society that transcends capitalism through working class struggles. The 'distinguishing feature of Communism is ... the abolition of bourgeois property', the '[a]bolition of private property' (MECW 6: 498). The role of machines in communism is in the *Manifesto* hinted at by the formulation that communism has to 'increase the total of productive forces as rapidly as possible' (MECW 6: 504). The concept of necessary labour-time and its technological reduction does not yet exist in the *Manifesto*. But it is clear that the establishment of 'an association, in which the free development of each is the condition for the free development of all' (MECW 6: 506) requires highly productive technologies that reduce the necessary labour-time to a minimum and enable a post-scarcity society.

So by the end of the 1840s, Marx and Engels had established a dialectical analysis of technology that stressed the antagonistic and class character of machinery's use in capitalism. They point out that capitalist technology is a means of increasing productivity and a means of control, rationalisation, globalisation and exploitation and is embedded into the antagonism between productive forces and relations of production. In the 1840s, Marx made clear that communism requires the abolition of private property and the division of labour, but he did not establish a clear understanding of the role of technology as one of the foundations of communism. Such a detailed analysis had to wait until Marx's work on the *Grundrisse* in the late 1850s.

3.4 THE 1850S: THE DISCOVERY OF SURPLUS-VALUE IN THE *GRUNDRISSE*

In 1859, Marx published *A Contribution to the Critique of Political Economy* (MECW 29: 257–417). At this point of time, he had already 'discovered' the category of surplus-value in 1857/58 when writing the *Grundrisse*, *Capital*'s first draft. *A Contribution ...* focuses only on the analysis of the commodity and money, but not capital, surplus-value and profit. Therefore, also the analysis of technology in capitalism as means of relative surplus-value production and fixed constant capital is missing. *A Contribution ...* does not contribute to the analysis of technology in capitalism. It was a rough draft of specific aspects of *Capital* that is mainly known for its *Preface* (MECW 29: 261–5), in which Marx summarises the dialectic of productive forces and relations of production. The language he uses for doing so operates at the level of the system of capitalism and neglects the subjects of labour as well as class struggle. Therefore, the impression can emerge that capital is an automatically developing and collapsing subject. Given that Marx in *A Contribution ...* does not focus on surplus-value, he does not solve the riddle of capitalist production, namely, that the working class' labour produces surplus-value that is transformed into monetary profit that the capitalist class appropriates.

In the *Grundrisse*, Marx in 1857/58 introduced the notion of surplus-value and along with it the concepts of necessary labour-time and surplus labour-time:

> The increase in the productive force of living labour increases the *value* of capital (or diminishes the value of the worker) not because it increases the quantity of products or use values created by the same labour – the productive force of labour is its natural force – but rather because it diminishes *necessary* labour, hence, in the same relation as it diminishes the former, it creates *surplus labour* or, what amounts to the same thing, surplus value; because the surplus value which capital obtains through the production process consists only of the excess of surplus labour over *necessary labour*. The increase in productive force can increase surplus labour – i.e. the excess of labour objectified in capital as product over the labour objectified in the exchange value of the working day – only to the extent that it diminishes the relation of *necessary labour to surplus labour*, and only in the proportion in which it diminishes this relation. Surplus value is exactly equal to surplus labour; the increase of the one [is] exactly measured by the diminution of *necessary labour*. (Marx 1857/58: 339)

Marx here describes a close relationship of surplus-value and technology in capitalism: Capital strives to increase unpaid labour-time in order to maximise profit. An important means for doing so is to increase productivity by making use of labour-saving technologies. As a consequence, the proportion of unpaid labour-time (surplus labour-time) increases and the proportion of the paid labour-time (necessary labour-time) decreases. The introduction of the category of surplus-value necessitates the distinction between necessary labour-time and surplus labour-time.

In the *Grundrisse*, Marx also introduces the distinction between constant and variable capital. He speaks of the 'division of capital into a constant part – raw material and instrument with an antediluvian existence before labour – and a variable part, that is, the necessary goods exchangeable for living labour capacity' (Marx 1857/58: 454). The value of constant capital does not increase, it is 'invariable value' (Marx 1857/58: 379) that is used up and transferred to the commodity in the capitalist production process. Human labour-power in contrast is put to work in the production process as labour that creates novel goods, new commodities and thereby new value. It therefore has a dynamic, variable character.

Furthermore, Marx introduces the distinction between fixed and circulating capital in the *Grundrisse*. Machinery is fixed capital because it is fixed in the production process for a longer time. It is not used up in the production of one commodity, but is used repeatedly as means for the production of many commodities over a longer time period. '[F]ixed capital, once it has entered the production process, remains in it' (Marx 1857/58: 680). '"Fixed capital" serves over and over again for the same, operation' (Marx 1857/58: 717). 'Fixed capital in its developed form hence only returns in a cycle of years which embraces a series of turnovers of circulating capital' (Marx 1857/58: 721).

In the *Grundrisse*, Marx introduces the two basic methods that capital uses for producing more surplus-value: (a) the absolute lengthening of the working day so that absolutely more unpaid labour-time is conducted; (b) the organisational change of the production process so that during the same the relation between paid and unpaid labour-time changes in such a way that the necessary labour-time decreases and surplus labour-time increases.

If we look at absolute surplus value, it appears determined by the absolute lengthening of the working day above and beyond necessary labour time. ... In the second form of surplus value, however, as relative surplus value, which appears as the development of the workers' productive power, as *the reduction of necessary labour time relative to the working day*, and *as the reduction of the necessary labouring population* relative to the population (this is the antithetical form), in this form there directly appears the industrial and the distinguishing historic character of the mode of production founded on capital. (Marx 1857/58: 661)

Whereas absolute surplus-value production has to do with primitive accumulation, the formal creation of wage-labour as legal relation and the creation of new realms of wage-labour (Marx 1857/58: 769–70), relative surplus-value production implies the transformation of the production process by new forms of technology and organisation. So in the *Grundrisse*, Marx establishes for the first time a clear relationship between the capitalist use of technology and the category of relative surplus-value production.

In the *Grundrisse*, Marx argues like in earlier works that capitalist technology alienates the worker. He, for example, writes that the '*automatic system of machinery*' and the capitalist use of science 'acts upon' the worker 'as an alien power' (Marx 1857/58: 692–3). A novel theoretical element is that Marx introduces the notion of the general intellect in the *Grundrisse*, by which he anticipated the emergence of an information economy:

The development of fixed capital indicates to what degree general social knowledge has become a *direct force of production*, and to what degree, then, the conditions of the process of social life itself have come under the control of the general intellect and been transformed in accordance with it. (Marx 1857/58: 706)

The basic argument is that capitalism requires the development of new technologies for increasing productivity. By doing so, it also introduces an increasing level of science and knowledge labour into the production process so that at a certain point of time the increase in quantity of science, knowledge and technology in production turns into a new quality – knowledge becomes a 'direct force of production', the knowledge economy emerges.

Marx expresses nowhere clearer than in the *Grundrisse* that communism requires highly productive technologies in order to abolish wage-labour and enable a society that is built around freely determined activities beyond compulsion and necessity. One of the manifold passages in the *Grundrisse*, where he expresses this fact, is the following one:

Real economy – saving – consists of the saving of labour time (minimum (and minimization) of production costs); but this saving identical with development of the productive force. ... The saving of labour time [is] equal to an increase of free time, i.e. time for the full development of the individual, which in turn reacts back upon the productive power of labour as itself the greatest productive power. (Marx 1857/58: 711)

By the end of the 1850s, Marx had fully developed the foundations of a critical theory of technology in the *Grundrisse*, including aspects of technology and alienation, the impact of the capitalist use of technology on society, the antagonism of productive forces and relations of production, technology and globalisation, technology and rationalisation, modern technology as fixed constant capital and method of relative surplus-value production, the general intellect, and technology in communism. The *Grundrisse* is a highly unsystematic work written in the form of notebooks. So the task that remained after the *Grundrisse* for a critical theory of technology was to turn its content into a more systematic form and to ground it in historical examples. Although these foundations had been established, Marx's main published economic work from the 1850s, *A Contribution to the Critique of Political Economy*, fell short of addressing technology because it focused on addressing the concepts of the commodity and money and did not establish a full critical theory of capital.

3.5 THE 1860S: FROM DRAFTS OF *CAPITAL* TO *CAPITAL VOLUME 1*

In the years 1861–63, Marx worked on another draft of *Capital*. The resulting manuscripts were in German published as the *Theories of Surplus Value* (volumes 26.1, 26.2 and 26.3 of the German *Marx-Engels-Werke* (MEW)) and the *Economic Manuscripts of 1861–63* (MEW volumes 43 and 44). In the English *Marx & Engels Collected Works*, Marx's works from the period 1861–63 are presented in the MECW volumes 30, 31, 32, 33 and 34. The *Theories of Surplus Value* are also sometimes seen as the fourth volume of *Capital* that elaborate Marx's critical assessment of classical political economy out of which he developed his approach as critique of political economy.

In a letter to Ferdinand Lasalle, dated 22 February 1858, Marx presents the six-book plan *Capital* with separate books on '1. On Capital (contains a few introductory CHAPTERS), 2. On Landed Property, 3. On Wage Labour, 4. On the State, 5. International Trade, 6. World Market' (MECW 40: 270). So at the time he wrote *Grundrisse*, he had this structure for the overall work in mind. By the mid-1860s, Marx had changed that structure into a four-volume plan: Marx first mentioned the four-book version in a letter to Engels dated 31 July 1865 (MECW 42: 173). In a letter to Ludwig Kugelmann (a German social democrat, who was a friend of both Marx and Engels and a member of the International Workingmen's Association), dated 13 October 1966, Marx fully sets out the four-book plan of *Capital*, where Volume 1 focuses on the production of capital, Volume 2 on the circulation of capital, Volume 3 on the structure of capital as a whole, and Volume 4 on the 'History of the Theory' (MECW 42: 328). The division into three volumes of *Capital* and the *Theories of Surplus Value* follows this suggested structure, although it is of course disputed what should and should not be included in Volumes 2 and 3 and the *Theories of Surplus Value* because Marx had died when these books were put together.

In the *Economic Manuscripts of 1861–63*, Marx introduces the concepts of the formal and real subsumption of capital under labour:

> Historically, in fact, at the start of its formation, we see capital take under its control (subsume under itself) not only the labour process in general but the specific actual labour processes as it finds them available in the existing technology, and in the form in which they have developed on the basis of non-capitalist relations of production. It finds in existence the actual production process – the particular mode of production – and at the beginning it only subsumes it *formally*, without making any changes in its specific technological character. Only in the course of its development does capital not only formally subsume the labour process but transform it, give the very mode of production a new shape and thus first create the mode of production peculiar to it. ... This *formal* subsumption of the labour process, the assumption of control over it by capital, consists in the worker's subjection as worker to the supervision and therefore to the command of capital or the capitalist. Capital becomes command over labour. (MECW 30: 92–3)

Formal subsumption means that wage-labour relations are imposed on particular forms of labour without transforming the mode of production. Real subsumption in contrast means a qualitative change of the mode of production so that more radical organisational and technological changes take place. Marx speaks of formal and real subsumption as '*two separate forms of capitalist production*' (MECW 34: 95). Formal and real subsumption for Marx correspond to forms of capitalist production that are based on absolute and relative surplus-value production: 'I call the form which rests on absolute surplus value the *formal subsumption of labour under capital.* ... The real subsumption of labour under capital is developed in all the forms which produce relative, as opposed to absolute, surplus value' (MECW 34: 95, 105).

In real subsumption, science and technology transform the production process qualitatively:

> With the real subsumption of labour under capital, all the CHANGES we have discussed take place in the technological process, the labour process, and at the same time there are changes in the relation of the worker to his own production and to capital – and finally, the development of the productive power of labour takes place, in that the productive forces of social labour are developed, and only at that point does the application of natural forces on a large scale, of science and of machinery, to direct production become possible. (MECW 34: 106)

In the *Economic Manuscripts of 1861–63*, Marx also again takes up the question of relative surplus-value production. 'In this case, therefore, where the surplus value cannot be raised any further by lengthening the overall working day, how can it be raised any further at all? By *shortening the necessary labour time*' (MECW 30: 233–4). Marx introduces three methods of relative surplus-value production (MECW 30: 255–346): co-operation, the division of labour in manufacturing, and machinery. The presentation is organised in the form of three sections. Each section presents one method of relative surplus-value production.

Co-operation has for Marx a general and a specific meaning. In general, it refers to 'the *collective labour of many workers*' (MECW 30: 255). Its more specific meaning is the '*agglomeration, heaping up of many workers in the same area* (in one place), all working *at the same time*' (MECW 30: 256). An example is that workers, who individually assemble toys from their homes, are amassed in a toy assemblage factory so that a foreman monitors them and speeds up the labour process. Marx here also speaks of 'simple cooperation' (MECW 30: 259). The second type is the division of labour within one workshop, the 'division of labour in the manufacture of a commodity' (MECW 30: 267) – the manufacture as a 'specific *mode of production*' (MECW 30: 268). In toy assemblage, this means that, for example, the first worker assembles the tail of a toy dog in the first step to the dog's body, the second the head, the third the left ear, the fourth the right ear, the fifth the snout, etc. The third type is the use of machinery. 'The purpose of machinery, speaking quite generally, is to lessen the value, therefore the price, of the commodity, to cheapen it, i.e. to shorten the labour time necessary for the production of a commodity' (MECW 30: 318).

These three sections form a direct draft of *Capital Volume I*'s fourth part 'The Production of Relative Surplus-Value', where the distinction of the three methods of relative surplus-value production is present in the form of three separate chapters that correspond to the three sections in the *1861–63 Economic Manuscripts*: Chapter 13 Co-operation (Marx 1867: 439–54), chapter 14: The Division of Labour and Manufacture (Marx 1867: 455–91), chapter 15: Machinery and Large-Scale Industry (Marx 1867: 492–639).

In the *Economic Manuscripts of 1861–63*, Marx also repeats the *Grundrisse*'s assumption that in capitalist development, knowledge becomes an immediate force of production:

> The employment of the *NATURAL AGENTS* – their incorporation so to speak into capital – coincides with the development of *scientific knowledge* as an independent factor in the production process. In the same way as the production process becomes an *application of scientific knowledge,* so, conversely, does science become a factor, a function so to speak, of the production process. (MECW 34: 32)

Marx here does not use the term general intellect, but instead speaks of 'scientific knowledge' (MECW 34: 32), '[s]cience' (MECW 34: 34) and 'the general intellectual product of social development' (MECW 34: 126).

In the parts of Marx's works from 1861–63 that were published as the *Theories of Surplus Value* (MEW 26.1, 26.2, 26.3; Marx 1963, 1969, 1972), he engages in detail with classical political economy in the works of James Steuart, Adam Smith, Jean Charles Léonard de Sismondi, Germain Garnier, Charles Ganilh, David Ricardo, James Frederick Ferrier, James

Maitland (Earl of Lauderdale), Jean-Baptiste Say, Destutt de Tracy, Henri Storch, Nassau Senior, Pellegrino Rossi, Thomas Chalmers, Jacques Necker, François Quesnay, Simon-Nicolas-Henri Linguet, Thomas Hobbes, William Petty, Dudley North, John Locke, David Hume, Joseph Massie, Louis-Gabriel Buat-Nançay, John Gray, Karl Rodbertus, John Barton, Nathaniel Forster, Thomas Hopkins, Henry Charles Carey, Thomas Robert Malthus, James Deacon, Thomas Hodgskin, James Anderson, Robert Torrens, James Mill, Samuel Bailey, John Ramsay McCulloch, Edward Gibbon Wakefield, Patrick James Stirling, John Stuart Mill, Piercy Ravenstone, John Francis Bray, Sir George Ramsay, Antoine-Eliseé Cherbuliez, Richard Jones, Pierre-Joseph Proudhon or Martin Luther. Machinery plays here and there a role in the discussion of particular theories, but there is no full chapter in the *Theories of Surplus Value* devoted just to machinery. Marx in *Capital* again and again refers to single elements from classical political economy. The *Theories of Surplus Value* show how Marx worked through classical political economy in order to develop a critique of it that led to *Capital*.

The *Results of the Immediate Process of Production* is a text of 130 printed pages that Marx wrote some time between June 1863 and December 1866 (Ernest Mandel's introduction, in Marx 1867: 944). It is printed as an appendix in the Penguin edition of *Capital Volume 1* (Marx 1867: 948–1084), but is not contained in the German *Marx-Engels-Werke* (MEW). In the *Results*, Marx again takes up the question of the formal and real subsumption of labour under capital and points out the importance of machinery as method of relative surplus-value production in the real subsumption of labour under capital:

> The general features of the *formal subsumption* remain, viz. the *direct subordination of the labour process to capital*, irrespective of the state of its technological development. But on this foundation there now arises a technologically and otherwise *specific mode of production – capitalist production* – which transforms the nature *of the labour process and its actual conditions*. Only when that happens do we witness the *real subsumption of labour under capital*. … The real subsumption of labour under capital is developed in all the forms evolved by relative, as opposed to absolute surplus-value. With the real subsumption of labour under capital a complete (and constantly repeated) revolution takes place in the mode of production, in the productivity of the

workers and in the relations between workers and capitalists. (Marx 1867: 1034–5)

Michael Hardt and Toni Negri have developed the concepts of the formal and real subsumption of labour under capital into the concepts of the formal and real subsumption of society under capital (Hardt & Negri 2009: 230, 2017: 178–82; Negri 1991: 131, 142). Formal subsumption means that non-capitalist relations and spheres play a formal role within capitalism. So, for example, housework is not organised as wage-labour but reproduces labour-power and is thereby productive, value-generating labour that (re-)creates the value of the commodity of labour-power. In the real subsumption of society under labour, formerly non-capitalist relations become directly commodified. Examples are the commodification of land, culture, nature, community, social relations, communication, the digital commons, etc.

David Harvey uses the term accumulation by dispossession for the phenomenon that Hardt/Negri term the real subsumption of society under capital. Accumulation by dispossession means the commodification of (almost) everything via privatisation, financialisation, the management and manipulation of crises, and state redistributions (Harvey 2005: 160–5). Accumulation by dispossession is for Harvey ongoing primitive accumulation of capital. 'All the features of primitive accumulation that Marx mentions have remained powerfully present within capitalism's historical geography up until now. ... Privatization (e.g. of social housing, telecommunications, transportation, water, etc. in Britain) has, in recent years, opened up vast fields for overaccumulated capital to seize upon' (Harvey 2003: 145, 149).

Whereas Harvey uses primitive accumulation for characterising the ongoing capitalist process of accumulation by dispossession based on Rosa Luxemburg, Hardt and Negri (2017: chapter 11) characterise primitive accumulation as capitalism's first development phase (that was followed by the phase of manufacture/large-scale industry and the phase of social production) and formal and real subsumption as ongoing processes. '*Marx's concept of "formal subsumption" provides a richer framework than primitive accumulation insofar as it reveals geographical and temporal differences and discontinuities by focusing on changes in production processes*' (Hardt & Negri 2017: 180).

Besides these formal differences in the use of Marxian categories, the real commonality of Harvey and Hardt/Negri is that they analyse how capitalism attempts to instrumentalise everything and turn it into commodities and under the logic of capital.

> *Primitive accumulation and formal and real subsumption help us articulate, then, how today's centrality of extraction in its various faces – from the extraction of oil and minerals to the financial capture of value produced through social cooperation and popular forms of life – does not indicate either a further step in a linear history or a cyclical return to the past.* (Hardt & Negri 2017: 182)

In the manuscripts written during the first half of the 1860s, Marx gave in respect to technology special attention to methods of relative surplus-value production, science in capitalist production, and the distinction between formal and real subsumption of labour under capital.

In *Capital Volume 1*, Marx (1867) devotes part 3 to 'The Production of Absolute Surplus-Value' (chapters 7–11), part 4 to 'The Production of Relative Surplus-Value' (chapters 12–15), and part 5 to 'The Production of Absolute and Relative Surplus-Value' (chapters 16–18). In chapter 16, Marx (1867: 645) mentions formal and real subsumption as absolute and relative surplus-value production, but this passage is much shorter than the exposition in the *Results of the Immediate Process of Production* and the *Economic Manuscripts of 1861–63*.

Capital Volume 1's chapter 15 'Machinery and Large-Scale Industry' is with 147 pages and ten sections not just *Capital*'s longest chapter, but also Marx's most detailed exposition of technology's role in capitalism (see Fuchs 2016d: chapter 15 for a detailed discussion). Marx defines capitalist machinery as fixed constant capital that is a means of relative surplus-value production.

> Machinery produces relative surplus-value, not only by directly reducing the value of labour-power, and indirectly cheapening it by cheapening the commodities that enter into its reproduction, but also, when it is first introduced sporadically into an industry, by converting the labour employed by the owner of that machinery into labour of a higher degree, by raising the social value of the article produced above its individual value, and thus enabling the capitalist to replace the value of a day's labour-power by a smaller portion of the value of a day's product. (Marx 1867: 530)

Marx stresses the dialectical, contradictory character of modern technology: It is as such a means for creating free time and wealth for all, but under capitalist conditions is a means for the exploitation and control of the workers that is embedded into the antagonism of productive forces and relations of production that generates crises. Marx builds his analysis of technology in capitalism on Hegel's dialectic of essence (technology-as-such) and existence (technology-in-capitalism):

> The contradictions and antagonisms inseparable from the capitalist application of machinery do not exist, they say, because they do not arise out of machinery as such, but out of its capitalist application! Therefore, since machinery in itself shortens the hours of labour, but when employed by capital it lengthens them; since in itself it lightens labour, but when employed by capital it heightens its intensity; since in itself it is a victory of man over the forces of nature but in the hands of capital it makes man the slave of those forces; since in itself it increases the wealth of the producers, but in the hands of capital it makes them into paupers, the bourgeois economist simply states that the contemplation of machinery in itself demonstrates with exactitude that all these evident contradictions are a mere semblance, present in everyday reality, but not existing in themselves, and therefore having no theoretical existence either. (Marx 1867: 568–9)

Marx in this passage also indirectly comes back to the issue of highly productive technology as the foundation of communism, but the exposition in the *Grundrisse* is certainly much more detailed. Marx remarks in *Capital* that the application of machinery would 'be entirely different in a communist society from what it is in bourgeois society' (Marx 1867: 515, footnote 33), whereby he indicates that one cannot simply apply old technologies without changes in a communist society, but that technology has to be re-designed along with the transformation of society.

In chapter 15, Marx also gives particular attention to machinery in the context of class struggles. Misery, precarity, crises and unemployment caused by capital and the capitalist use of technology result in 'periodic revolts of the working class against the autocracy of capital' (Marx 1867: 562). But machinery is also 'the most powerful weapon for suppressing strikes' (Marx 1867: 562). While communism is more a theme in the *Grundrisse* than *Capital Volume 1*, there is more focus on class struggles in the latter work than in the first. Class struggles in capitalism are struggles about labour-time and wages. In *Capital Volume 1*, Marx gives particular attention to struggles for the shortening of the working day. So, for example, he reports that 'the gradual upsurge of working-class revolt had compelled Parliament compulsorily to shorten the hours of labour, and to begin by imposing a normal working day on factories' (533). But such struggles are ambivalent because

> from the moment that it was made impossible once and for all to increase the production of surplus-value by prolonging the working day, capital threw itself with all its might, and in full awareness of the situation, into the production of relative surplus-value, by speeding up the development of the machine system. (Marx 1867: 534)

Chapter 15 is not just theoretical, but also empirical in character. Marx uses reports of factory inspectors in order to document and analyse the situation of labour under the conditions of large-scale capitalist industry. So, for example, he talks about the effects of the introduction of sewing machines:

> The new machine-minders are exclusively girls and young women. ... The new female workers turn the machines by hand and foot, or by hand alone, sometimes sitting, sometimes standing, according to the weight, size and special make of the machine, and expend a great deal of labour-power. Their occupation is unwholesome, owing to the long hours, although in most cases these are not so long as under the old system. Wherever the sewing-machine is located in narrow and already over-crowded workrooms, it adds to the unwholesome influences. (Marx 1867: 601–2)

If one substitutes in such passages the word 'sewing machine' by 'assemblage of computer technologies in China', then one gets a description of how working conditions today look like in the Chinese Foxconn factories (see Qiu 2016). In the age of digital capitalism, workers still face the issue of long hours, precarious labour, surveillance, control and high levels of exploitation.

3.6 CONCLUSION

This chapter traced the development of Marx's concept of technology in the 1840s, 1850s and 1860s. It reread Marx by showing the genealogy of one of his concepts. Marx's most sustained analysis of technology can be found in *Capital Volume 1*'s chapter 15 and the *Grundrisse*'s *Fragment on Machines*. We have, however, seen that technology has from the 1840s been an important concept for Marx that he also addressed in works such as the *Economic and Philosophic Manuscripts*, *The German Ideology*, *The Poverty of Philosophy*, the *Manifesto of the Communist Party*, *Wage Labour and Capital*, the *Economic Manuscripts of 1861–63* and the *Results of the Immediate Process of Production*. Engels' early works such *as The Condition of England* and *The Condition of the Working-Class in England* certainly influenced Marx's thoughts on technology's role in capitalism.

Taken together, we can identify the following elements of Marx's critical theory of technology:

- *Dehumanisation*: Capitalism dehumanises individuals by treating them like dead things, resources and machines.
- *Alienation*: The capitalist use of machines is embedded into the alienation of the workers so that they become appendages to the machine. Capitalist technology has a class and alienated character.
- *Fixed constant capital*: In capitalism, technology is fixed constant capital and one of the means of relative surplus-value production and control.
- *Relative surplus-value production*: Co-operation, the division of labour and machinery are three important methods of relative surplus-value production.
- *The real subsumption of labour under capital*: The distinction of formal and real subsumption of labour under capital discern among two forms of capitalist production. In the second one, technology plays a crucial role as means of relative surplus-value production that qualitatively transforms the production process.
- *The antagonism of the productive forces and the relations of production*: The capitalist use of technology is embedded into and advances the contradiction between the productive forces and the relations of production that is one of the sources of capitalist crises. Modern technology creates an antagonism between necessary labour-time and surplus labour-time that creates one of the foundations of communism and well-rounded individuality, but within capitalist class relations is one of the sources of crisis, precarious labour, unemployment, overwork and the uneven distribution of labour-time.

- *The general intellect*: The development of modern technology in the context of capitalism's drive to increase productivity results at a specific point of time in the emergence of an information economy, in which the general intellect – science and knowledge in production – has become a direct productive force.
- *The division of labour*: Capitalist technology is embedded into the class division of labour that results in divisions such as the international division of labour, the gender division of labour, the urban and rural division of labour, the division of labour within one unit of production, the division of labour between labour and management, the division of labour between mental and manual labour, etc.
- *Social problems*: The capitalist use of machinery contributes to social problems such as overwork, unemployment, stress, workplace injuries, precarious labour, work surveillance, etc.
- *Technology and class struggles*: Technology does not determine society, but is rather embedded into class struggles. Technology is not the cause, but a means and result of social and societal change. The application of modern technology is contested and its impacts are subject to the outcome of class struggles.
- *Contradictions of technology, the dialectic of technology and society*: Technology in capitalism has contradictory effects on the economy and society.
- *Technology and communism*: Communism requires highly productive technologies in order to abolish wage-labour and enable a post-scarcity society that is built around freely determined activities beyond compulsion and necessity.

A key insight of Marx's theory of machines is that technology is in capitalism contradictory and embedded into society's dialectics and social struggles. The effects of technology on society are not pre-determined, but depend on the outcomes of class struggles. Figure 3.1 visualises this dialectic character of technology.

Marx distinguishes between the technology as means of production (see this chapter) and means of communication (see Chapter 4). Today, this distinction has become blurred. The networked computer is a convergence technology that is a means of communication and a means of production and a digital machine that enables the production, distribution and consumption of information with one and the same technology.

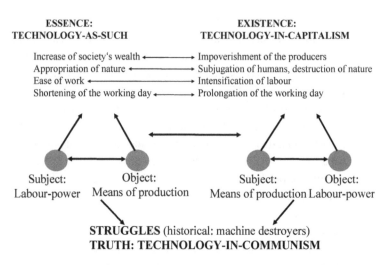

Figure 3.1   Technology's contradictory character

The computer is a universal machine, it is not just a medium of communication but also an instrument of production for the production of digital goods, information (e.g. user-generated content), communication and social relations.

The contemporary sociology of digital technologies has since the rise of the computer been dominated by a gap between technological optimists and technological pessimists, technological determinists and social constructionists, theories of technological structuralism and technological agency. All of these epistemologies, ontologies and axiologies of technologies are one-dimensional and deeply flawed. They lack a Marxian understanding of the contradictory character of contemporary technologies, the dialectic of technology and society, and the embeddedness of technology into class and social struggles.

Digital machines have within digital capitalism become a new fetishism of technology that can be observed as ideologies of the Internet and ideologies on the Internet. Ideologies of the Internet either over- or underestimate the role of digital media in society by considering it as either determining society and being the cause of everything good or everything bad or as a factor of communication that is superstructural, secondary and unimportant in society. Ideologies on the Internet are online expressions of ideologies (such as nationalism, racism, fascism, technological determinism, instrumental reason, neoliberalism, etc.) that aim at manipulating, distorting and dissimulating presentations of reality so that they do not correspond to actual reality and legitimate exploitation and domination. The contemporary prevalence of fake news is an example.

In the age of digital capitalism, we can learn from Marx's critical theory of technology that mobile phones, the Internet, social media, data, robotics, artificial intelligence, digital automation and other digital technologies are not evil as such, but at the same time also do not automatically bring about a better society. Digital communism requires democratic and participatory forms of digital media that enable the reduction of necessary labour-time to a minimum, a maximum of free time and a democratic public sphere. Digital media need to be shaped in democratic ways together and embedded into the creation of a participatory democracy in order to form the foundation of a truly democratic society. This means that we require the fundamental transformation of digital capitalism via social struggles and radical reforms so that a participatory digital democracy, a society of the digital and social commons, is not just a hope, but an active hope that we long for not just in our dreams, but also in our political practices.

4

Rereading Marx as Critical Theorist of Communication

4.1 INTRODUCTION

The date 5 May 2018 marked Karl Marx's bicentenary. He was born on 5 May 1818. One hundred years later, the German socialist and historian Franz Mehring, author of one of the first biographies of Karl Marx (Mehring 1936/2003), wrote on the occasion of Marx's centenary:

> Karl Marx's centenary directs our view from a gruesome presence to a brighter future just like a bright sunbeam that breaks through dark and apparently impenetrable cloud layers … Tireless and restless critique … was his true weapon. … To continue working based on the indestructible foundations that he laid is the most worthy homage we can offer to him on his one hundredth birthday.[1] (Mehring 1918: 11, 15)

Given the gruesome present we live in today that features the expansion and intensification of nationalisms and neo-fascisms, the threat of a new World War, environmental, economic and political crises, Mehring's words are as true on the occasion of Marx's bicentennial just like they were 100 years ago.

Marx was first and foremost a critic and critical theorist, which entailed that he was a critical economist, critical philosopher, critical political scientist, critical sociologist, critical journalist and revolutionary activist. The task of this contribution on the occasion of Marx's

---

1 Translated from German. German original: 'Wie ein heller Sonnenstrahl, der durch düstere und scheinbar undurchdringliche Wolkenschichten bricht, so lenkt heute der hundertste Geburtstag von Karl Marx unseren Blick aus einer grauenvollen Gegenwart in eine hellere Zukunft … die rast- und ruhelose Kritik … ist seine wirkliche Waffe gewesen … . So fortzuarbeiten auf den unzerstörbaren Grundlagen, die er gelegt hat, ist die würdigste Huldigung, die wir … [ihm] an seinem hundertsten Geburtstage darbringen können.'

bicentenary is to show that he was also a critical communication scholar. This circumstance has often been forgotten in radical theory because communication is often ignored or dismissed as being an unimportant superstructure.

This chapter shows in three steps how Marx's works can ground a critical theory of communication: Section 4.2 introduces aspects of communicative materialism. Section 4.3 discusses means of communication and communicative labour. Section 4.4's focus is on foundations of ideology critique. Section 4.5 draws conclusions.

4.2 COMMUNICATION'S MATERIALITY: DIALECTICAL, CRITICAL, COMMUNICATIVE MATERIALISM

In the *Theories of Surplus Value*, Marx speaks of the existence of 'non-material production' (Marx 1861–63: 143) that entails the production of books and paintings, artistic creation, writers, engineers, the work of 'executant artists, orators, actors, teachers, doctors, clerics, etc.' (144). In a newspaper article, he speaks of privileges as '*immaterial* goods' (Marx 1848: 477). In the *Grundrisse*, Marx argues that value is 'something *immaterial*, something indifferent to its material consistency' (Marx 1857/58: 309).

According to these assumptions, information and its production are not part of the 'material base', but of the 'superstructure'. Such a dichotomy between materiality and immateriality can indeed be found in particular versions of Marxist thought. So, for example, the *Small Dictionary of Marxism-Leninism* defines the superstructure as 'ideas (political, legal, cultural, scientific, ideological, moral, artistic ones)' (Buhr & Kosing 1979: 46). It understands the superstructure as the '*ideological* societal relations of a societal formation' (Buhr & Kosing 1979: 46) and consistently speaks of 'institutional and ideal contents' (47). The problem is that the question about matter is one about the world's substance and ground. If one assumes that there is something immaterial in the world, then there must be two substances – matter and spirit. The implication then is not just religious and esoteric, namely, that spirit exists as a substance in the universe, but the human mind is also seen as independent from matter.

Marx does, however, not frequently use the concept of immateriality. He mainly employs it in drafts. In *Capital*, he in contrast says that 'the ideal is nothing but the material world' translated in 'the mind of man' and into 'forms of thought' (Marx 1867: 102). He also writes about 'the intellectual potentialities [*geistige Potenzen*] of the material process of production' (Marx 1867: 482). In *The German Ideology*, Marx says that the 'production of ideas, of conceptions, of consciousness, is at first directly interwoven with the material activity and the material intercourse of men – the language of real life' (Marx & Engels 1845/46: 36). The mind 'is from the outset afflicted with the curse of the being "burdened" with matter' (Marx & Engels 1845/46: 43–4).

Taken together, these formulations imply that information and communication are forms of matter and that the production of information is part of the material production process. When Marx speaks of the 'material intercourse of men', then, he not only describes the human thought process, but how humans in the communication process co-relate their thoughts and thereby produce a new whole. By stressing that communication is 'the language of real life', Marx foregrounds that information and communication are not unreal or immaterial, but part of humans' production and reproduction processes in everyday life.

But just like communicative idealism that sees communication as a superstructure, also a vulgar communicative materialism should be avoided. Stalin's writings on linguistics are an ideal-type of vulgar communicative materialism: Language 'radically differs from the superstructure. Language is not a product of one or another base, old or new, within the given society, but of the whole course of the history of the society and of the history of the bases for many centuries' (Stalin 1972: 5). Language is

> common to all members of that society, as the common language of the whole people. Hence the functional role of language, as a means of intercourse between people, consists not in serving one class to the detriment of other classes, but in equally serving the entire society, all the classes of society. (Stalin 1972: 5–6)

> Language, on the contrary, is connected with man's productive activity directly, and not only with man's productive activity, but with all his other activity in all his spheres of work, from production to the base, and from the base to the superstructure. ... For this reason the sphere of action of language, which embraces all fields of man's activity, is far broader and more comprehensive than the sphere of action of the superstructure. (Stalin 1972: 9)

Language, as a means of intercourse, always was and remains the single language of a society, common to all its members. (Stalin 1972: 20)

Stalin's writings on language fulfilled an ideological purpose: He wanted to stress that language is the constituting feature of the nation. In *Marxism and the National Question*, Stalin (1913: 306) stresses, for example, that 'a common language is one of the characteristic features of a nation'. Instead of seeing its ideological and dominative character, Stalin reified the nation.

The humanist Marxist Leo Kofler (1970) criticised Stalin's approach to language as reductionist and mechanistic:

Stalin primarily notices language's emblematical technical, *phonetic-morphological* side, i.e. its relatively *fixed* side. However, his dialectically untrained eye is not capable of seeing what has inadequately been called the 'stylistics', but can better be termed language's *'life'* as the fully valid and true essence of language. His writing completely neglects this side of language. But this 'life' constitutes the *ideological* and therefore *changing* moment of language, or, better expressed, the ideological and therefore *necessarily* changeable moment of language. Technology and life of language are related to each other like form and content.[2] (Kofler 1970: 135–6)

Kofler's point is that Stalin only focuses on the syntax and technology of language and leaves out its use, contents, semantics and pragmatics. A dialectical approach to language needs to take into account its formal and semantic side, aspects of technology and culture, the economic and non-economic, etc.

A small number of approaches that are today widely ignored, forgotten or undiscovered have within Marxist theory stressed the material character of communication. Raymond Williams points out

---

2   Translated from German. Original: 'Stalin bemerkt an der Sprache vornehmlich nur ihre zeichenhaft technische, ihre *phonetisch-morphologische*, also ihre relative *starre* Seite. Hingegen ist sein dialektisch ungeschultes Auge nicht in der Lage, das, was man sehr unzulänglich die "Stilistik", etwas besser das *"Leben"* der Sprache bezeichnet hat, in ihrer vollgültigen, ja das wahre Wesen der Sprache ausmachenden Bedeutung zu erkennen. In seiner Schrift wird diese Seite der Sprache vollkommen vernachlässigt. In diesem "Leben" liegt aber das *veränderliche*, weil *ideologische*, oder besser das ideologische und deshalb *zwangsläufig* veränderliche Moment der Sprache. Technik und Leben der Sprache verhalten sich zueinander wie Form und Inhalt.'

that many Marxist approaches separate the economy and culture and are not 'materialist enough' (Williams 1977: 92, 97). It is idealist to separate '"culture" from material social life' (Williams 1977: 19). In such idealist approaches, 'intellectual and cultural production ... appear to be "immaterial"' (Williams 1989: 205). Williams criticises approaches that separate matter and ideas either temporally by arguing that first comes 'material production, then consciousness, then politics and culture' or spatially by assuming that there are levels and layers built on the economic base (Williams 1977: 78). Language and communication are material practices of production (165). Williams speaks of 'the material character of the production of a cultural order' (93; for a detailed discussion of how the communication concept is related to Williams' cultural materialism, see Fuchs 2017b).

Georg Lukács (1986a, 1986b) argues with his concept of teleological positing that goal-oriented production is the key feature of humans and society. Language and communication are for Lukács key features of society, a complex that enables the social reproduction of society (for a detailed discussion, see Fuchs 2016a: chapter 2). Ferruccio Rossi-Landi (1983) stressed the work-character of communication (see Fuchs 2016a: chapter 6). Horst Holzer (1975: 30) stresses that 'humans *produce communicatively* and *communicate productively*' (see Fuchs 2017a).

Such approaches foreground the material character of communication, which means that communication is the material production and reproduction process of social relations, social systems, organisations, groups, institutions, subsystems, society and sociality. Communication is at the same time identical and non-identical with the economy and the work process: Just like all production, communication is purposeful: It aims at creating social relations. But communication also has a differentia specifica that makes it different from other work processes: It creates and spreads meanings and therefore is a meaning-making production and work process.

Figure 4.1 shows the relationship of the economic and the non-economic. Communication is a process that spans across both realms.

That communication is a particular type of production is one of its important features. But it is not just production, but social production. We do not produce and communicate alone and in isolation, like Robinson Crusoe on his island, but in company, in common and in processes of co-operation. Marx stresses the social character of communication:

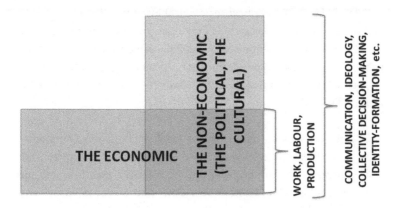

Figure 4.1   The relation of the economic and the non-economic in society

Language is as old as consciousness, language *is* practical, real consciousness that exists for other men as well, and only therefore does it also exist for me; language, like consciousness, only arises from the need, the necessity, of intercourse with other men. Where there exists a relationship, it exists for me: the animal does not 'relate' itself to anything, it does not 'relate' itself at all. For the animal its relation to others does not exist as a relation. Consciousness is, therefore, from the very beginning a social product, and remains so as long as men exist at all. (Marx & Engels 1845/46: 44)

That communication and language are social also means that humans develop, create and communicate names for instances of being because 'they use these things in practice, ... these things are useful to them' (Marx 1881: 539).

At a certain stage of evolution after their needs, and the activities by which they are satisfied, have, in the meanwhile, increased and further developed, they will linguistically christen entire classes of these things which they distinguished by experience from the rest of the outside world. ... Thus: human beings actually started by appropriating certain things of the outside world as means of satisfying their own needs, etc. etc.; later they reached a point where they *also* denoted *them linguistically* as what they are for them in their practical experience, namely as *means of satisfying their needs*, as things which 'satisfy' them. (Marx 1881: 539)

One of Marx's main critical sociological insights is that in capitalism and society in general, everything existing in and is constituted through social relations: The commodity, capital, capitalism, labour, money, value, classes, exploitation, domination, social struggles, communism, etc. are social relations. Marx in this context compares humans to the commodity:

> In a certain sense, a man is in the same situation as a commodity. As he neither enters into the world in possession of a mirror, nor as a Fichtean philosopher who can say 'I am I', a man first sees and recognizes himself in another man. Peter only relates to himself as a man through his relation to another man, Paul, in whom he recognizes his likeness. With this, however, Paul also becomes from head to toe, in his physical form as Paul, the form of appearance of the species man or Peter. (Marx 1867:144, footnote 19)

Marx here stresses that the human species and the human being are constituted through social relations. By making a metaphorical comparison to the commodity, he neither means that all social relations are instrumental and aimed at profit nor that social relations are a form of exchange. He rather stresses that the commodity as social relation reveals something about capitalism and society in general. In commodity exchange, buyer and seller relate to each other and exchange products (such as money and certain goods) as equals that were created under specific social conditions. A quantitative relationship of exchange is established. At the same time, any commodity exchange just like any other social relation has general features of human sociality such as the use of means, content, meanings, context and impacts of communication.

Social relations need to be produced and reproduced. Communication is the production and reproduction process of social relations and therefore of society. Marx stresses that language and communication are social relations and that they constitute social relations. Society is possible because it is based on the social character of language and communication and the communicative character of social relations.

> Not only is the material of my activity given to me as a social product (as is even the language in which the thinker is active): my *own* existence *is* social activity, and therefore that which I make of myself,

I make of myself for society and with the consciousness of myself as a social being. (Marx 1844c: 298)

Production by an isolated individual outside society – a rare exception which may well occur when a civilized person in whom the social forces are already dynamically present is cast by accident into the wilderness – is as much of an absurdity as is the development of language without individuals living together and talking to each other. (Marx 1857/58: 84)

As regards the individual, it is clear e.g. that he relates even to language itself as his own only as the natural member of a human community. Language as the product of an individual is an impossibility. But the same holds for property. Language itself is the product of a community, just as it is in another respect itself the presence [Dasein] of the community, a presence which goes without saying. (Marx 1857/58: 490)

Figure 4.2 shows a model of communication as social production process: Humans through communication produce the social that enters

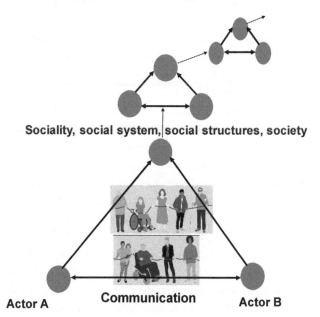

Figure 4.2   Model of communication as social production process

into new communication processes so that sociality is an open totality. Humans produce and reproduce the social (including social relations, social structures, social systems, groups, organisations, institutions, subsystems, society) and the (re-)produced social structures again and again enter new communication processes that in a self-reflexive manner create and re-create social structures. Expressed differently, one can say that society is a realm constantly emerging out of the dialectic of structures and human agency, in which communication is the productive process of mediation and in which humans co-produce social structures that enable and constrain human action so that the dialectic constantly dynamically reproduces itself, human sociality, social structures and society. Communication is the productive mediating process that organises the dialectic of structure and agency as open totality.

Marx not only analysed the communication process, but also the role of the means of communication and cultural/communicative labour in capitalism.

4.3 THE MEANS OF COMMUNICATION AND COMMUNICATIVE LABOUR IN CAPITALISM

In *Capital Volume 1*'s technology chapter 'Machinery and Large-Scale Industry', Marx (1867) advances a dialectical concept of technology. He stresses that capitalist technology has a contradictory character: It advances new potentials for co-operation and welfare for all, but is under capitalist conditions also a means of exploitation and domination. Capitalist technology is ambivalent, ambiguous and contradictory (for a detailed discussion, see Fuchs 2016d: chapter 15). Marx's dialectical approach to technology and society allows us today, in the age of social media, big data, the Internet of Things, cloud computing, mobile communication, industry 4.0, artificial intelligence, etc., to avoid techno-optimism that celebrates every innovation and is uncritical about negative impacts as well as techno-pessimism that fights technology as such and wants to return to a society without modern technology that is shaped by toil. The point of progressive technology and communications politics is to appropriate, transform, re-design, re-shape the means of production and the means of communication as particular means of production into a progressive direction, which requires societal change along with technological transformation.

So Marx, on the one hand, stresses the dominative role of capitalist technology: 'Every development of new productive forces is at the same time a weapon against the workers. All improvements in the means of communication, for example, facilitate the competition of workers in different localities and turn local competition into national, etc.' (Marx 1847: 423).

[N]o improvement of machinery, no appliance of science to production, no contrivances of communication, no new colonies, no emigration, no opening of markets, no free trade, nor all these things put together, will do away with the miseries of the industrious masses; but that, on the present false base, every fresh development of the productive powers of labour must tend to deepen social contrasts and point social antagonisms. (Marx 1864: 9)

On the other hand, Marx argues that modern technologies can be appropriated and transformed. So, for example, he writes that the worker's 'appropriation of his own general productive power' (Marx 1857/58: 705) has the potential to foster 'the general reduction of the necessary labour of society to a minimum, which then corresponds to the artistic, scientific etc. development of the individuals in the time set free, and with the means created, for all of them' (Marx 1857/58: 706).

Marx stresses that there is a dialectic of society's temporal and spatial aspects and the development of technology and communications (= the means of communication). Technologies do not develop arbitrarily. In class societies, their emergence is shaped by particular interests and power structures. At the same time, technology development and use is not determined, but also has a degree of unpredictability.

Capitalism reaches spatial and temporal limits that it tries to overcome in order to avoid crisis and continue accumulation. 'Capital is the endless and limitless drive to go beyond its limiting barrier' (Marx 1857/58: 334). Capital accumulation requires: (1) labour-power; (2) means of production (raw materials, technologies, infrastructure); (3) commodity markets; (4) capital and capital investment. Globalisation and imperialism are strategies to cheapen the access to labour-power and means of production, as well as to gain access to new commodity markets and opportunities for capital export and capital investment. New transport and communication technologies are the medium and outcome of the globalisation of capitalism: The

> revolution in the modes of production of industry and agriculture made necessary a revolution in the general conditions of the social process of production, i.e. in the means of communication and transport. ... the means of communication and transport gradually adapted themselves to the mode of production of large-scale industry by means of a system of river steamers, railways, ocean steamers and telegraphs. (Marx 1867: 505–6)

It is no accident that the Internet became so important in a new phase of the globalisation of capitalism.

The globalisation of production lengthens the turnover time of capital, the total time it takes to produce and sell commodities, because the commodities have to be transported from one place to another. As a consequence, capitalism strives to develop technological innovations in transport and communications in order to speed-up the production and distribution of commodities and the circulation of capital. 'Economy of time, to this all economy ultimately reduces itself' (Marx 1857/58: 173).

Capitalism is shaped by the drive to expand and accumulate capital and power. Capitalism's inherent imperialistic character requires that the exploitation of labour, commodity sales and political rule are organised across spatio-temporal distances. Capitalism therefore advances the development of technologies that allow the organisation of capitalism by traversing long spatial distances in a short time. In addition, there is a capitalist tendency of acceleration. Acceleration is based on the principle of accumulating more economic, political and cultural power in less time. Acceleration means that more commodities are produced and consumed, more decisions made and more experiences organised in ever less time. As a tendency, the capitalist logic of accumulation calls forth processes of acceleration, globalisation and financialisation as capitalist strategies and what David Harvey (2003) terms temporal, spatial and spatio-temporal fixes that aim at temporarily overcoming capitalism's inherent crisis tendencies. 'The spatio-temporal "fix" ... is a metaphor for a particular kind of solution to capitalist crises through temporal deferral and geographical expansion' (Harvey 2003: 115). Capitalism tends to defer crises geographically and into the future, but again and again reaches its limits that express themselves as crises.

The development of new technologies is embedded into the search for spatio-temporal fixes to capitalism's immanent crisis tendencies.

The transport of humans, information and commodities is a key feature of capitalism. The means of transport and the means of communication therefore play a significant role in the organisation of accumulation. The following quotes show the importance that Marx gives to the phenomenon of the 'shortening of time and space by means of communication and transport' (Marx 1865: 125):

> If the progress of capitalist production and the consequent development of the means of transport and communication shortens the circulation time for a given quantity of commodities, the same progress and the opportunity provided by the development of the means of transport and communication conversely introduces the necessity of working for ever more distant markets, in a word, for the world market. The mass of commodities in transit grows enormously, and hence so does the part of the social capital that stays for long periods in the stage of commodity capital, in circulation time – both absolutely and relatively. A simultaneous and associated growth occurs in the portion of social wealth that, instead of serving as direct means of production, is laid out on means of transport and communication, and on the fixed and circulating capital required to keep these in operation. (Marx 1885: 329)

> The main means of cutting circulation time has been improved communications. (Marx 1894: 164)

> The more production comes to rest on exchange value, hence on exchange, the more important do the physical conditions of exchange – the means of communication and transport – become for the costs of circulation. Capital by its nature drives beyond every spatial barrier. Thus the creation of the physical conditions of exchange – of the means of communication and transport – the annihilation of space by time – becomes an extraordinary necessity for it. Only in so far as the direct product can be realized in distant markets in mass quantities in proportion to reductions in the transport costs, and only in so far as at the same time the means of communication and transport themselves can yield spheres of realization for labour, driven by capital; only in so far as commercial traffic takes place in massive volume – in which more than necessary labour is replaced – only to that extent

is the production of cheap means of communication and transport a condition for production based on capital, and promoted by it for that reason. (Marx 1857/58: 524–5)

Marx not only describes the importance of the means of communication in capitalism, but also how the production of knowledge and communication develops due to capitalism's need to increase productivity. Increasing productivity requires scientific progress and expert knowledge in production. The rising importance of knowledge and communicative labour is a consequence of the capitalist development of the productive forces. Marx in the *Grundrisse* anticipated the emergence of what some today term informational capitalism or digital capitalism or cognitive capitalism. He speaks in this context of the general intellect: 'The development of fixed capital indicates to what degree general social knowledge has become a direct force of production, and to what degree, then, the conditions of the process of social life itself have come under the control of the general intellect and been transformed in accordance with it' (Marx 1857/58: 706).

Also in *Capital*, Marx stresses the importance of the communication industry for capitalism. He argues that the 'communication industry' that focuses on 'moving commodities and people, and the transmission of mere information – letters, telegrams, etc.' is 'economically important' (Marx 1885: 134). He writes that there are capitalists who 'draw the greatest profit from all new development of the universal labour of the human spirit' (Marx 1894: 199). Today, these capitalists are CEOs, managers and shareholders of transnational communication corporations such as Apple, AT&T, Verizon, Microsoft, China Mobile, Alphabet/Google, Comcast, Nippon, Softbank, IBM, Oracle, Deutsche Telekom, Amazon, Telefónica, etc.

Theories of the information society, whose ideal-type is Daniel Bell's (1976) approach, claim that information production has become dominant in the economy and has radically transformed society into a new formation. Marxists are often critical of such claims that entail the danger of overlooking and downplaying the continuities of capitalism. Consequently, neoliberal ideologues often celebrate new technologies as radically transforming everything towards the better. But in wanting to avoid technological determinism and idealism, Marxists often simply ignore the role of communication technologies and information production in the economy and society. The point is that today we experience the interaction of many capitalisms, including digital capitalism, communicative capitalism, finance capitalism, mobility capitalism, hyper-industrial capitalism, etc. (Fuchs 2014a: chapter 5).

Autonomist Marxism, especially the version advanced by Michael Hardt and Antonio Negri, is based on the notion of Marx's general intellect and stresses the rise of knowledge in capitalism. 'General intellect is a collective, social intelligence created by accumulated knowledges, techniques, and knowhow. The value of labor is thus realized by a new universal and concrete labor force through the appropriation and free usage of the new productive forces. What Marx saw as the future is our era' (Hardt & Negri 2000: 364). 'Just as in a previous era Lenin and other critics of imperialism recognized a consolidation of international corporations into quasi-monopolies (over railways, banking, electric power, and the like), today we are witnessing a competition among transnational corporations to establish and consolidate quasi-monopolies over the new information infrastructure' (Hardt & Negri 2000: 300). Hardt and Negri are among the limited number of radical theorists who have taken the role of communication in capitalism seriously.

Marx was also visionary in respect to the emergence of the Internet. He envisioned a system that enables establishing 'interconnections', where 'each individual can acquire information about the activity of all others and attempt to adjust his own accordingly', and 'connections are introduced thereby which include the possibility of suspending the old standpoint' (Marx 1857/58: 161). Doesn't Marx here give a perfect description of the Internet? Can we say that Karl Marx invented the Internet?

Another important contribution that Marx made to ground foundations of a critical theory of communication is his critique of ideology.

4.4 IDEOLOGY AS FETISHISED COMMUNICATION, FETISHISM AS IDEOLOGICAL COMMUNICATION

Marx critically theorised ideology and practised the ideology critique of religion, bourgeois thought and capitalism. In his very early works, he stressed that ideologies create illusions and deceive and criticised religion as ideology:

Religion is the sigh of the oppressed creature, the heart of a heartless world, just as it is the spirit of spiritless conditions. It is the *opium* of the people. To abolish religion as the *illusory* happiness of the people is to demand their *real* happiness. The demand to give up illusions about the existing state of affairs is the *demand to give up a state of affairs which needs illusions*. (Marx 1844b: 175–6)

For Marx, the belief in religion is an ideological expression of a dominative society. He criticised left-wing thinkers such as Bruno Bauer and Ludwig Feuerbach for stopping at the critique of religion and not seeing how it is related to capitalism and necessitates the critique of capitalism. For Marx, 'the criticism of heaven' has to turn 'into the criticism of the earth, the *criticism of religion* into the *criticism of law* and the *criticism of theology* into the *criticism of politics*' (Marx 1844b: 176).

The German Ideology is a draft book that Marx and Engels wrote for gaining self-understanding of the contemporary German philosophy and left-wing critique of their time. In *The German Ideology*, Marx argues that in 'all ideology men and their relations appear upside-down as in a *camera obscura*' and that 'this phenomenon arises just as much from their historical life-process as the inversion of objects on the retina does from their physical life-process' (Marx & Engels 1845/46: 36). It here becomes evident that Marx conceives ideology based on Hegel's dialectic of essence and appearance: Ideologies make existence appear different from how it really is. It hides the true essence and state of the world behind false appearances and communicates these false appearances as truths and nature. Ideology makes being appear as immediate, but illusionary reality whose simplicity hides the underlying complexity of the world that cannot always be experienced directly. Hegel (1991: addition to §112) argues that the 'immediate being of things is … represented as a sort of rind or curtain behind which the essence is concealed'. For Hegel, the truths hidden behind appearances are part of the world's logic. In contrast, for Marx the process of hiding, naturalising, concealing and making truth disappear is an immanent expression of and practice in class societies.

In *Capital*, Marx (1867: 163–77) developed the insight that ideology hides power relations and naturalises domination into the concept of commodity fetishism. The commodity is a 'mysterious' and 'a very strange thing' (Marx 1867: 163).

The mysterious character of the commodity-form consists therefore simply in the fact that the commodity reflects the social characteristics of men's own labour as objective characteristics of the products of labour themselves, as the socio-natural properties of these things. Hence it also reflects the social relation of the producers to the sum total of labour as a social relation between objects, a relation which exists apart from and outside the producers. Through this substitution, the products of labour become commodities, sensuous things which are at the same time supra-sensible or social. (Marx 1867: 164–5)

The very structure of capitalism makes commodities, capital, money, classes, etc. appear as natural properties of society. Because of the division of labour and the mediated character of capitalism, producers and consumers do not directly experience the whole production process of the commodity. In everyday capitalist life, we are primarily confronted with commodities and money as things, whereas the production process and its class relations remain hidden. Capitalism is thereby in itself ideological in the very practices of capitalist production. Fetishism is ideological just like ideology is fetishist: Ideology fetishises certain changeable social relations as static, unchangeable, natural, thing-like entities.

The commodity is bound up with a peculiar capitalist form of language and communication: 'Commodities as such are indifferent to all religious, political, national and linguistic barriers. Their universal language is price and their common bond is money' (Marx 1859: 384). In *Capital*, Marx argues that the commodity's price (the monetary expression of a commodity's average value) and value are the commodity's language:

We see, then, that everything our analysis of the value of commodities previously told us is repeated by the linen itself, as soon as it enters into association with another commodity, the coat. Only it reveals its thoughts in a language with which it alone is familiar, the language of commodities. In order to tell us that labour creates its own value in its abstract quality of being human labour, it says that the coat, in so far as it counts as its equal, i.e. is value, consists of the same labour as it does itself. In order to inform us that its sublime objectivity as a value differs from its stiff and starchy existence as a body, it says that value has the appearance of a coat, and therefore that in so far as the linen itself is an object of value [*Wertding*], it and the coat are as like as two peas. Let us note, incidentally, that the language of commodities also has, apart from Hebrew, plenty of other more or less correct dialects. The German word 'Wertsein' (to be worth), for instance, brings out less strikingly than the Romance verb 'valere', 'valer', 'valoir' that the equating of commodity B with commodity A is the expression of value proper to commodity A. (Marx 1867: 143–4)

Price information communicates the value of a commodity. Capitalism has its particular form of capitalist communication, in which things appear to speak to humans. The sales process is a dehumanised form of communication, in which humans do not interact with each other, but the commodity speaks to humans through its price and advertising. The commodity form is a capitalist medium of communication that because of its fetishist character hides the social relations and power structures in which humans communicatively produce and productively communicate and constitute and reproduce class relations and exploitation. The commodity form is a reifying and fetishistic form of communication that speaks to humans in categories of things and prices of things. Horst Holzer (1975: 45) stresses in this context that the 'communicative character of commodities and the commodity character of communication' form the 'foundation of an illusory synthesis at the level of society as a whole.'[3] The commodity form not only communicates prices, but also communicates that the commodity and capital are the natural organisation forms of society as a whole. Given the reified and alienated status of the commodity in capitalism, the commodity form of communication (advertising as audience/user commodity, communicative labour-power as commodity, access to information and communication as commodities, communicative contents as commodities, communication technologies as commodities, etc.) can also appear as natural properties of communication.

'The social relations of production embedded in goods are systematically hidden from our eyes. The real meaning of goods, in fact, is emptied out in capitalist production and consumption' (Jhally 2006: 88). Capitalist production through the fetishism of commodities empties out the real meaning of commodities and renders the real communication processes and their power structures that organise commodity production invisible. Advertising is a form of fetishised communication

---

3 Translation from German. German original: Der 'Kommunikativ-Charakter der Waren und der Warencharakter der Kommunikation' sind die 'Basis einer scheinhaften gesamtgesellschaftlichen Synthese'.

that produces and communicates artificial meanings of commodities. 'Production empties. Advertising fills' (Jhally 2006: 89). Advertising is so powerful because it tells commodity stories and provides meanings about goods and the economy. It uses various strategies for doing so, for example, black magic, a commodity communication strategy, where 'persons undergo sudden physical transformations' or 'the commodity can be used to entrance and enrapture other people' (Jhally 2006: 91). 'The real function of advertising is not to give people information but to make them feel good' (Jhally 2006). Advertising is a secular form of religion, a magic communication system (Williams 1980). Advertising is a system of commodity fetishism: It promises satisfaction and happiness through the consumption of things (Jhally 2006: 102). Advertising is propaganda that promotes the ideology of human happiness through consumption of commodities. But advertising is not just a form of ideo- logical communication that acts as commodity propaganda. It is also a peculiar commodity itself that is produced through the exploitation of audiences' and users' labour that creates attention and data (Fuchs 2014a, 2015b; Smythe 1977).

In his *Comments on James Mill's 'Elements of Political Economy'*, Marx (1844a) makes clear that the language of commodities is not a true form of communication, but an alienated and alienating type of communication characteristic for capitalism. In capitalism, language and communication are ideologically deformed, fetishising and naturalising:

> The only intelligible language in which we converse with one another [in capitalism] consists of our objects in their relation to each other. We would not understand a human language and it would remain without effect. By one side it would be recognised and felt as being a request, an entreaty, and therefore a *humiliation*, and consequently uttered with a feeling of shame, of degradation. By the other side it would be regarded as *impudence* or *lunacy* and rejected as such. We are to such an extent estranged from man's essential nature that the direct language of this essential nature seems to us a *violation of human dignity*, whereas the estranged language of material values seems to be the well-justified assertion of human dignity that is self-confident and conscious of itself. (Marx 1844a: 227)

For Marx, the fetishist character of language and communication in capitalism is not limited to the economy, but extends itself into the realms of politics and culture, where the state, bureaucracy, the ruling parties, the nation, nationalism, wars, racism, etc. appear through ideologies as natural forms of human communication and society. So whereas an economic form of ideology operates in the commodity's and capital's social form, we also find political ideologies in capitalism that act in a fetishist manner and in doing so aim at justifying dominant group's rule and distract attention from how capitalism and domination are at the heart of inequalities and other problems of society.

The most significant ideological and societal shift that societies around the world face today is the emergence of new nationalisms. In contemporary capitalism, neoliberal capitalism has turned into new authoritarian capitalisms signified by new nationalisms and political phenomena such as Donald Trump (USA), Brexit (UK), Recep Tayyip Erdoğan (AKP, Turkey), Viktor Orbán (Fidesz, Hungary), Heinz Christian Strache (Freedom Party, Austria), Norbert Hofer (Freedom Party, Austria), Sebastian Kurz (Austrian People's Party), the Alternative for Germany (Germany), Narendra Modi (Bharatiya Janata Party, India), Rodrigo Duterte (PDP-Laban, Philippines), Marine Le Pen (National Front, France), Geert Wilders (Party for Freedom, the Netherlands), Nigel Farage (UK Independence Party), Jarosław Kaczyński (Law and Justice Party, Poland), Andrej Babiš (Action of Dissatisfied Citizens, Czech Republic), the Finns Party (Finland), Golden Dawn (Greece), Jobbik (Hungary), the Danish People's Party, the Sweden Democrats, etc. The analysis of new forms of authoritarian capitalism is a key task for a Marxist theory of communication and ideology today. It has to involve an analysis of the structure of ideology, the way ideology is communicated over various media, including not just traditional ones (newspapers, speeches, television, radio), but also mobile media, social media and the Internet, its societal causes, and social struggles that could constitute alternatives.

Features of right-wing authoritarianism include hierarchic leadership, the friend/enemy-scheme, patriarchy, and the belief in militarism and law and order as means for responding to conflicts (Fuchs 2018). Right-wing authoritarian ideology involves the presentation of refugees, immigrants, foreigners, foreign states or other groups as enemies of the nation that threaten its social cohesion and/or culture. Nationalism is an ideology that constructs a fictive national unity of capital and labour by opposing the nation to a foreign enemy and thereby distracts attention from how social problems are grounded in class, exploitation and domination. Nationalism is a 'misty veil' that 'conceals in every case a definite historical content' (Luxemburg 1976: 135). Nationalism is a political fetishism that communicates the nation in the form of a 'we'-identity (a national people) that is distinguished from enemies (outsiders, other nations, immigrants, refugees, etc.) that are presented as intruders, aliens, sub-humans, parasites, uncivilised, etc.

Marx did not limit the analysis of ideology and fetishism to the economy, but also criticised political fetishisms such as nationalism. So, for example, in 1870, he discussed the role of nationalism in distracting attention from class struggle and benefiting the ruling class. He analysed the creation of false consciousness among the working class in one country so that it hates immigrant workers and workers in the colonies. He specifically addressed that question in respect to Ireland as a British colony:

Ireland is the BULWARK of the *English landed aristocracy.* The exploitation of this country is not simply one of the main sources of their material wealth; it is their greatest *moral* power. ... And most important of all! All industrial and commercial centres in England now have a working class *divided* into two *hostile* camps, English PROLETARIANS and Irish PROLETARIANS. The ordinary English worker hates the Irish worker as a competitor who forces down the STANDARD OF LIFE. In relation to the Irish worker, he feels himself to be a member of the *ruling nation* and, therefore, makes himself a tool of his aristocrats and capitalists *against Ireland,* thus strengthening their domination *over himself.* He harbours religious, social and national prejudices against him. ... This antagonism is kept artificially alive and intensified by the press, the pulpit, the comic papers, in short by all the means at the disposal of the ruling class. *This antagonism* is the *secret of the English working class's impotence,* despite its organisation. It is the secret of the maintenance of power by the capitalist class. And the latter is fully aware of this. (Marx 1870: 473, 474, 475)

For Marx, overcoming ideology requires overcoming capitalism, class society, exploitation and domination.

4.5 CONCLUSION

In Marx's works, there are a number of important elements of a critical theory of communication, including the following ones:

- Communication is a material process in which humans produce and reproduce social relations, social structures, social systems, groups, organisations, institutions, society and sociality.
- Society is possible because it is based on the social character of language and communication and the communicative character of social relations.
- Communication has both economic and non-economic features.
- Marx opposed technological determinism by a dialectic of technology and society that sees technology (including the means of communication) as having a contradictory character in class societies.
- Technologies do not develop arbitrarily. In class societies, their emergence is shaped by particular interests and power structures. At the same time, technology's development and use are not determined, but also have a degree of unpredictability.
- Marx stressed that there is a dialectic of society's temporal and spatial aspects and the development of technology and communications (= the means of communication).
- With the notion of the general intellect, Marx anticipated the emergence of communicative/informational/digital/cognitive capitalism.
- Marx critically theorised ideology as a fetishist form of communication. Ideology hides the true essence and state of the world behind false appearances and communicates these false appearances as truths and nature.
- Capitalism has its particular form of capitalist communication, in which things appear to speak to humans. The sales process is a dehumanised form of communication, in which humans do not interact with each other, but the commodity speaks to humans. The language of commodities is not a true form of communication, but an alienated and alienating type of communication characteristic for capitalism.
- The fetishist character of language and communication in capitalism is not limited to the economy, but extends itself into

the realms of politics and culture, where the state, bureaucracy, the ruling parties, the nation, nationalism, wars, racism, etc. appear through ideologies as natural forms of human communication and society.

Struggles for socialist alternatives are struggles for 'the *positive* transcendence of *private property as human self-estrangement*', 'the real *appropriation* of the *human* essence by and for man', 'the complete return of man to himself as a *social* (i.e., human) being', 'humanism', 'the true resolution of the strife between existence and essence, between objectification and self-confirmation, between freedom and necessity, between the individual and the species' (Marx 1844c: 296).

Such a society would be a true communication society, in which social relations would not be shaped by asymmetric power structures and exploitation, but controlled by the community of humans who act, produce, decide and live in common based on the common control of society. Commons-based communication means to make something common to a community. It is a process of commoning.

The term communication in modern language is derived from the Latin verb *communicare* and the noun *communicatio*. *Communicare* means to share, inform, unite, participate, and literally to make something common. A heteronomous and class-divided society is a society based on particularistic control. Struggles for the commons in contrast aim at overcoming class and heteronomy and to make society a realm of common control. In an economy of the commons, the means of production are owned collectively. In a polity of the commons, everyone can directly shape and participate in collective decision-making. In a culture of the commons, everyone is recognised. In such a participatory democracy, humans speak and communicate as a common voice. They own and decide together and give recognition to each other.

A communicative society is not a society in which humans communicate because humans have to communicate in all societies in order to survive. A communicative society is also not an information society in which knowledge and information/communication technologies have become structuring principles. A communicative society is a society in which the original meaning of communication as making something common is the organising principle. Society and therefore also communication's existence then correspond to communication's essence. A communicative society is a society controlled in common so that communication is sublated and turned from the general process of the production of sociality into the very principle on which society is founded. A communicative society also realises the identity of *communicare* (communicating, making common) and *communis* (community). Society becomes a community of the commons. Such a society is a commonist society. Commons-based media enable communication whose *'primary freedom ... lies in not being a trade'* (Marx 1842: 175).

5

Rereading Marx in the Age of Digital Capitalism: The Case of Industry 4.0 and the Industrial Internet as the Digital German Ideology

5.1 INTRODUCTION: WHAT IS INDUSTRY 4.0?

In the past five years, there has been much talk in the world of digital media about 'industry 4.0' and the 'industrial Internet' as constituting the fourth industrial revolution. Especially in Germany, a vivid public debate has emerged about 'Industrie 4.0' that has featured government strategies and investments, white papers, reports, studies, the formation of an industry interest group (Plattform Industrie 4.0, see www.plattform-i40. de), public debates, research projects, a multitude of publications, etc. (see, e.g., Aichholzer et al. 2015; Austrian Institute of Technology, WIFO & Fraunhofer Austria Research 2017; Bitkom 2015; Bundesminsterium für Arbeit und Soziales 2015; Bundesministerium für Bildung und Forschung 2013; Bundesministerium für Wirtschaft und Energie 2015; Forschungsunion Wirtschaft – Wissenschaft & Deutsche Akademie der Technikwissenschaften 2013; Holtgrewe et al. 2015; Spath et al. 2013). German corporations involved in industry 4.0 include SAP, Siemens, Software AG, Wincor Nixdorf, Psipenta, Seeburger, CA, Bosch, Felten AG, KUKA and Festo AG.

What is industry 4.0? It is a concept that propagates the combination of the Internet of Things, big data, social media, cloud computing, sensors, artificial intelligence, robotics, and the application of the combination of these technologies to the production, distribution and use of physical goods. Cyber-physical systems are embedded computing systems that are applied to industrially produced components: Chips are embedded into manufactured goods so that they can be networked and connected to the Internet. The networking of humans through social media and the generation of big data is extended to machines so that networks of communicating machines are created. In the most extreme case, industry 4.0 means that a good is fully automatically produced, delivered, used, repaired and recycled without human intervention through the networking of different technologies over the Internet. The German Federal Ministry of Education and Research argues that in industry 4.0, 'equipment, machines and single components continuously exchange information' so that 'in the future many processes will be controlled and coordinated in real time over large distances' (Bundesministerium für Bildung und Forschung 2013: 6). The result are smart factories and smart products.

This chapter outlines a Marxist perspective on industry 4.0. Section 5.2 recapitulates Marx's position on automation. Section 5.3 argues that the fourth industrial revolution ('industry 4.0') is an ideology. Section 5.4 outlines the political economic reasons of why German capital seeks to advance industry 4.0. Section 5.5 outlines ten reasons why one should be sceptical of industry 4.0. Section 5.6 draws some conclusions.

5.2 MARX AND MARXISTS ON AUTOMATION

The application of the computer in capitalist economies has since the 1960s resulted in Marxist analyses of computerised forms of automation. Harry Braverman, André Gorz and David F. Noble made influential contributions to the Marxist debate on automation.

5.2.1 Harry Braverman: Automation and the Degradation of Labour

Harry Braverman (1974/1998) argues that automation has resulted in the degradation of labour in the twentieth century. Degradation includes deskilling, dequalification, proletarianisation, rising unemployment, surveillance and control. Braverman summarises his basic insight as follows:

> Thus the tendency of the capitalist mode of production from its earliest days some 200 or 250 years ago to the present, when this tendency has become a headlong rush, is the incessant breakdown of labor processes into simplified operations taught to workers as tasks. This leads to the conversion of the greatest possible mass of labor into work of the most elementary form, labor from which all conceptual elements have been removed and along with them most of the skill,

knowledge, and understanding of production processes. Thus the more complex the process becomes, the less the worker understands. The more science is incorporated into technology, the less science the worker possesses; and the more machinery that has been developed as an aid to labor, the more labor becomes a servant of machinery. (Braverman 1974/1998: 319)

Braverman (1974/1998: 324) ascertains an increase of unemployment as a consequence of automation in the twentieth century: 'The most striking thing to emerge from an examination of the unemployment statistics from the Second World War to the present is the long-run trend of gradual but persistent enlargement of the pool of officially counted unemployed.'

The computer as automation technology has, according to Braverman, advanced the degradation of labour. An example would be the computerisation of the office and white-collar labour: 'The computer system working on these principles is the chief, though not the only, instrument of mechanization of the office' (226). 'And with the economies furnished by the computer system and the forcing of the intensity of labor come layoffs which selectively increase the tendency toward factory-like work' (231). White-collar labour in the age of computerisation would see 'the creation of a large proletariat in a new form' (245).

5.2.2 André Gorz: Automation and Post-Industrial Socialism

Whereas Braverman focuses predominantly on the analysis of negative effects of automation within capitalism, André Gorz (1982) has a much more optimistic view of automation technologies. Gorz agrees with Braverman's analysis that computerisation and automation under capitalist conditions have negative effects for the workforce: 'Automation and computerisation have eliminated most skills and possibilities for initiative and are in the process of replacing what remains of the skilled labour force (whether blue or white collar) by a new type of unskilled worker' (Gorz 1982: 28). 'Mechanisation has given rise to the fragmentation and dequalification of work and made it possible to measure work according to purely quantitative standards' (38). 'The fragmentation of work, taylorism, scientific management and, finally, automation have succeeded in abolishing the trades and the skilled workers whose "pride in a job well done" was indicative of a certain consciousness of their practical sovereignty' (46).

Going beyond Braverman, Gorz also stresses the possibility that 'the time spent on heteronomous labour is to be reduced to a minimum' so that 'the mass of socially necessary labour' is 'distributed among the population as a whole in such a way that the average working day reduced to a few hours' (101).

Gorz argues for the reduction of socially necessary labour-time by automation, the creation of free time used for non-market activities in self-managed co-operatives that use alternative technologies, and the creation of a basic income guarantee. He calls this utopia post-industrial socialism. Such a society is based on the principle 'Work less, live more!' (134).

Only with capitalism does work, or the heteronomous production of exchange-values, become a full-time activity and the self-supply of goods and services (by the family or community) become a marginal and subordinate activity. An inversion of this relationship will signify the end of political economy and the advent of 'post-industrial socialism' or communism. (Gorz 1982: 82)

Gorz argues for 'the abolition of work', by which he understands the 'suppression of the need to purchase the right to live (which is almost synonymous with the right to a wage) by alienating our time and our lives' (2). 'It is possible to enlarge the non-market field of autonomous, self-managed and self-motivated activity, encouraging auto-centred production and training, and replacing some of the services currently supplied by commercial organisations or bureaucratic administrations with mutual aid, cooperation and sharing' (98).

Gorz maintains that the political goal of the Left should not be a society with 'full employment', but 'a society in which everyone is entitled to the satisfaction of his or her needs in return for an amount of socially necessary labour occupying only a small fraction of a lifetime' (123). In such a society, 'alternative technologies' are used 'to do more, better and with less, while at the same time increasing the autonomy of individuals and local communities' (124). Each 'individual is to be guaranteed a lifelong social income in return for 20,000 hours of socially useful work' (124).

Gorz (1989) imagines the emergence of a realm of autonomous activities in a post-industrial socialist society. This realm is no longer characterised by instrumental economic reason.

Non-working time is no longer necessarily time for the rest, recuperation, amusement and consumption ... If the working week were reduced to under twenty-five or thirty hours, we *could* fill our disposable time with activities which have no economic objective and which enrich the life of both individual and group: cultural and aesthetic activities whose aim is to give and create pleasure and enhance and 'cultivate' our immediate environment; assistance, caring and mutual-aid activities which create a network of social relations and forms of solidarity throughout the neighbourhood or locality; the development of friendships and affective relationships; educational and artistic activities; the repairing and production of objects and growing food for our own use, 'for the pleasure' of making something ourselves, of preserving things we can cherish and hand down to our children; service-exchange co-operatives, and so on. In this way it will be possible for an appreciable proportion of the services currently provided by professionals, commercial enterprises or public institutions to be provided on a voluntary basis by individuals themselves, as members of grassroots communities, according to needs they themselves have defined. (Gorz 1989: 233–4)

Nick Srnicek and Alex Williams[1] (2015) have continued Gorz's approach in a techno-optimistic manner. They argue for advancing full automation together with a politics that brings about a postcapitalist society as a world without work. 'The newest wave of automation is creating the possibility for huge swathes of boring and demeaning work to be permanently eliminated' (Srnicek & Williams 2015: 1–2).

The dreams of space flight, the decarbonisation of the economy, the automation of mundane labour, the extension of human life, and so on,

---

1   Paul Mason (2015) in his book *PostCapitalism* provides another version of the analysis of automation and technology that is comparable to the ones presented in this section (Braverman, Gorz, Noble). He argues that computerised automation and the Internet have resulted in zero-cost products and the destruction of capitalism's economic value-base so that a new long wave of economic growth cannot emerge and capitalism must collapse. Mason's approach resembles Henryk Grossmann's (1929/1992) breakdown theory of capitalism (see Fuchs 2016c for details).

are all major technological projects that find themselves hampered in various ways by capitalism. The boot-strapping expansionary process of technology, once liberated from capitalist fetters, can potentiate both positive and negative freedoms. It can form the basis for a fully postcapitalist economy, enabling a shift away from scarcity, work and exploitation, and towards the full development of humanity. (Srnicek & Williams 2015: 179)

5.2.3 David F. Noble: Automation and Class Struggle

The Marxist historian of technology David F. Noble studied the history of automation from the nineteenth century until the phase of computerised automation. According to Noble, computerised automation constitutes the second industrial revolution and under capitalist conditions results in crises and instability:

These latest devices give capital a new mobility, enabling capitalists to pick and choose from the world's reservoir: societies and peoples played off against one another in search of the cheapest and most servile hands. Moreover, these new technical systems hold out the prospect not simply of making robots out of people, but of substituting robots for people and dispensing with the need for human labour altogether – all in the name of economic and technological progress. No wonder, then, that this second transition, like the first, is marked by social instability and economic crisis, 'with the demand for work and workers equally diminished'. (Noble 1995: 44)

Second industrial revolution, computerised automation:

As a result, we see, not the revitalization of the nation's industrial base but its further erosion; not the enlargement of resources but their depletion; not the replenishing of irreplaceable human skills but their final disappearance; not the greater wealth of the nation but its steady impoverishment; not an extension of democracy and equality but a concentration of power, a tightening of control, a strengthening of privilege; not the hopeful hymns of progress but the somber sounds of despair, and disquiet. (Noble 1984/2011: 353)

Noble questions the 'ideology of technological progress, according to which technological advance is viewed as being inescapably beneficial for society' (Noble 1984/2011: 351). He argues for advancing an alternative vision of society through class struggles. His position is essentially a form of Marxism that stresses the need of class struggles for humanising society. 'It is essential to dream alternative dreams, to hold out a vision of a more humane future, but to believe that, under present political conditions, these technologies might be turned to humane ends is a dangerous delusion' (Noble 1984/2011: 351). Social struggles for alternatives have to challenge the ideology of technological progress:

> The problem is political, moral, and cultural, as is the solution: a successful challenge to a system of domination which masquerades as progress. Such a challenge will no doubt require opposition to technology in its present form – to buy time and cripple the current attack. And it will require political mobilization and vision, cultural inventiveness and rejuvenation, and a revitalization of moral confidence. But it will also require once and for all a transcendence of the irrational and infantile ideology of technological progress which has confounded Western thinking for at least two centuries – an ideology which has for too long obscured the realities of power in society, provided legitimation and cultural sanction for those who wield it, and paralyzed any and all opposition. (Noble 1984/2011: 351)

5.2.4 Marx on Automation

Braverman, Gorz and Noble have applied Marx's theory to twentieth-century automation technologies. Marx influenced their thought in different ways. But what did Marx himself say about automation?

The work process consists of a sequence of actions. The higher the share of actions in the production process that are performed by machines, the higher is the level of automation. Marx stresses that automation means that a machine carries out operations independent of human action in the labour process:

> As soon as a machine executes, without man's help, all the movements required to elaborate the raw material, and needs only supplementary assistance from the worker, we have an automatic system of machinery, capable of constant improvement in its details. Such improvements as

the apparatus that stops a drawing frame whenever a sliver breaks, and the self-acting stop which stops the power-loom as soon as the shuttle bobbin is empty of weft, are quite modern inventions. (Marx 1867: 503)

In a comparable manner to Marx, Friedrich Pollock argues: 'The aims and methods of automation may be provisionally defined as a technique of production the object of which is to replace men by machines in operating and directing machines as well as in controlling the output of the products that are being manufactured' (Pollock 1957: 5).

In *Capital Volume 1*, Marx stresses that the capitalist use of technology aims at controlling workers and substituting their labour-power by automated machinery. As a result, machines and automation are in capitalism tools of domination:

Along with the tool, the skill of the worker in handling it passes over to the machine. The capabilities of the tool are emancipated from the restraints inseparable from human labour-power. This destroys the technical foundation on which the division of labour in manufacture was based. Hence, in place of the hierarchy of specialized workers that characterizes manufacture, there appears, in the automatic factory, a tendency to equalize and reduce to an identical level every kind of work that has to be done by the minders of the machines. (Marx 1867: 545)

Every kind of capitalist production, in so far as it is not only a labour process but also capital's process of valorization, has this in common, but it is not the worker who employs the conditions of his work, but rather the reverse, the conditions of work employ the worker. However, it is only with the coming of machinery that this inversion first acquires a technical and palpable reality. Owing to its conversion into an automaton, the instrument of labour confronts the worker during the labour process in the shape of capital, dead labour, which dominates and soaks up living labour-power. (Marx 1867: 548)

In *Capital Volume 1*, Marx gives an analysis of automation that has influenced Braverman and the Bravermanian tradition of labour-process analysis. The question he asks is: How does automation substitute, dehumanise, alienate and control the worker?

In the *Grundrisse*, *Capital*'s first draft, Marx gives a definition of auto-mation that is similar to the one that can be found in *Capital Volume 1*:

> But, once adopted into the production process of capital, the means of labour passes through different metamorphoses, whose culmi-nation is the machine, or rather, an automatic system of machinery (system of machinery: the automatic one is merely its most complete, most adequate form, and alone transforms machinery into a system), set in motion by an automaton, a moving power that moves itself; this automaton consisting of numerous mechanical and intellectual organs, so that the workers themselves are cast merely as its conscious linkages. (Marx 1857/58: 692)

On the one hand, Marx in the *Grundrisse* describes just like in *Capital* how automation acts in capitalism as technology of control:

> Rather, it is the machine which possesses skill and strength in place of the worker, is itself the virtuoso, with a soul of its own in the mechanical laws acting through it … The worker's activity, reduced to a mere abstraction of activity, is determined and regulated on all sides by the movement of the machinery, and not the opposite. The science which compels the inanimate limbs of the machinery, by their construction, to act purposefully, as an automaton, does not exist in the worker's consciousness, but rather acts upon him through the machine as an alien power, as the power of the machine itself. (Marx 1857/58: 693)

But, on the other hand, Marx in the *Grundrisse* also advances the notion of the communist appropriation of machinery, including automation technology. Capitalism is based on capital's appropriation of human labour mediated by technology (objectified labour):

> The appropriation of living labour by objectified labour – of the power or activity which creates value by value existing for-itself – which lies in the concept of capital, is posited, in production resting on machinery, as the character of the production process itself, including its material elements and its material motion. The production process has ceased to be a labour process in the sense of a process dominated by labour as its governing unity. (Marx 1857/58: 693)

Modern technology forms the heart of capitalism's antagonism between productive forces and relations of production. This antagonism simultaneously advances crises tendencies and the emergence of communist potentials that stem from the socialisation of labour. In contrast to capitalist appropriation, communist appropriation means that 'individuals ... are associated on the basis of common appropriation and control of the means of production' (Marx 1857/58: 159).

In the *Fragment of Machines*, which forms a part of the *Grundrisse*, Marx describes the emergence of an information economy as the consequence of the development of capitalism's productive forces. He argues that due to the development of the productive forces a phase has to come, 'general social knowledge' that he also terms the 'general intellect' has become 'a *direct force of production*' (Marx 1857/58: 706). Marx anticipates a computerised society.

Only in such a society, it becomes possible to minimise human toil and necessary labour-time so that a realm of freedom, in which humans are freely active by being independent of coerced labour and wage-labour, emerges.

It is capital's tendency '*to create disposable time, on the other, to convert it into surplus labour*' (Marx 1857/58: 708). Under capitalist conditions, automation tends to foster unemployment and precarious labour, on the one hand, accompanied by overwork, on the other hand. There is a capitalist antagonism between necessary and surplus labour-time. It can only be overcome through class struggles that aim at a society, where the 'mass of workers ... themselves appropriate their own surplus labour' (Marx 1857/58: 708).

> Once they have done so – and disposable time thereby ceases to have an antithetical existence – then, on one side, necessary labour time will be measured by the needs of the social individual, and, on the other, the development of the power of social production will grow so rapidly that, even though production is now calculated for the wealth of all, disposable time will grow for all. For real wealth is the developed productive power of all individuals. The measure of wealth is then not any longer, in any way, labour time, but rather disposable time. (Marx 1857/58: 708)

So, in the *Grundrisse*, Marx also stresses the element that is characteristic for the works of André Gorz, namely, the communist potentials of modern technologies for the abolition of toil and the reduction of socially necessary labour-time. This position asks: How could technology be a humanist force in a communist society? How can technology advance communist potentials? A communist society is a society shaped by free time as the true source of wealth:

> Real economy – saving – consists of the saving of labour time (minimum (and minimization) of production costs); but this saving identical with development of the productive force. ... The saving of labour time [is] equal to an increase of free time, i.e. time for the full development of the individual, which in turn reacts back upon the productive power of labour as itself the greatest productive power. (Marx 1857/58: 711)

For Marx, free time is not leisure-time because leisure presupposes a sphere of alienated labour from which one has to escape. Rather, free time is freely determined time beyond necessity. Communism is, as Marx (1894: 959) argues in *Capital Volume 3*, the 'true realm of freedom, the development of human powers as an end in itself'. It begins beyond the realm of necessity. 'The reduction of the working day is the basic prerequisite' (Marx 1894: 959). 'Behind all the inhuman aspects of automation as it is organized under capitalism, its real possibilities appear: the genesis of a technological world in which man can finally withdraw from, evacuate, and oversee the apparatus of his labor – in order to experiment freely with it' (Marcuse 1968/2009: xxiii).

Marx's analysis of automation is dialectical. He neither welcomes nor rejects automation as such, but argues that the character, form, shaping, use and effects of automation depend on power relations. In capitalist society, capitalists will try to use automation for advancing their profit interests. Given that capitalism is a society in which profit interests have to stand over human interests and human life, capitalists have to accept and foster precarious work, precarious life, inequalities, unemployment, etc. in order to advance capital accumulation. Marx advances neither a positive nor a negative analysis and assessment of automation, but a dialectical position that stresses that automation is in capitalism embedded into the antagonisms between productive forces/relations or production and necessary labour-time/surplus-labour-time. He fosters a class struggle perspective on automation. This means that the question about automation's consequences is one that depends on the results of class struggles.

Taking a Marxian perspective on the newest wave of automation technologies, namely, those having to do with artificial intelligence, big data, cloud computing, social media and the Internet of Things, consequently means that we need to explain these technologies based on the analysis of class struggles today. Such struggles include the attempt of the bourgeois class to find ever newer methods of increasing and intensifying the appropriation of surplus-value. A class struggle perspective also stresses the importance of workers, unions, social movements and parties devising class struggles from below that aim at driving back the power of capital and aim at appropriating the means of production, including the newest technologies. Such a communist appropriation aims at transforming, alternatively shaping, alternatively designing and alternatively using technologies. It aims at establishing technologies of the commons, that is, technologies that are owned, controlled and operated in a self-managed manner by the immediate producers, and produce benefits for all. Common technologies require and point towards a society of the commons. The goal of a socialist politics of technology and automation is 'to integrate automation with a free and democratic society. Success in such planning would mean ... to establish a social system based upon reason' (Pollock 1957: 253).

5.3 THE FOURTH INDUSTRIAL REVOLUTION AS NEW IDEOLOGY

The argument advanced by the mainstream debate goes that industry 4.0 is the fourth industrial revolution that follows on from technological revolutions brought about by water and steam power (industrial revolution 1.0), electric power (industrial revolution 2.0) and computing/computerised automation (industrial revolution 3.0) (see Figure 5.1 for a visualisation of this claim).

One should always be sceptical about claims that revolutions will inevitably take place soon. So, for example, a study by the Fraunhofer Institute for Industrial Engineering claims that 'the fourth industrial revolution will have revolutionary impacts on production in Germany' (Spath et al. 2013: 134). Such claims are not just technological determinist (technology is seen as determining economic development) and ignore aspects of class struggle and political economic development, but

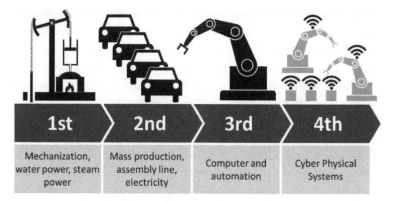

Figure 5.1 Industry 4.0, by ChristophRoser, AllAboutLean.com, CC BY-SA 4.0, via Wikimedia Commons

also proclaim a revolution before it has taken place. The idea of a technological revolution comes in this version before actual technological and economic developments. Industry 4.0 is the attempt to talk a new technological paradigm ideologically into existence.

Industry 4.0 is an ideology that promises economic growth: The German Federal Ministry for Economic Affairs and Energy estimates that within a ten-year period there is a market potential of industry 4.0 technologies (Internet of Things, digital intelligence, robotics, cloud computing) in Germany of almost 45 trillion euros (Bundesministerium für Wirtschaft und Energie 2015: 8). The figure is based on surveys. It neither takes into account investment and maintenance costs that reduce actual profits nor that industry representatives tend to use surveys as a marketing tool and therefore tend to overestimate potential positive economic effects.

5.4 THE POLITICAL ECONOMY BACKGROUND OF THE INDUSTRY 4.0 IDEOLOGY

Why is there so much talk about industry 4.0 now? And why in Germany? In the USA, the share of manufacturing in value-added decreased from 23.3 per cent in 1970 to 12.3 per cent in 2015. In the UK, there was a decrease from 27.0 per cent to 9.8 per cent. In Germany, manufacturing's share of value-added is in contrast almost 25 per cent, whereas the share of the FIRE sector and information and communication industries is significantly lower than in the USA and the UK (Table 5.1). Germany has a somewhat less financialised and significantly more manufacturing-based economy than the USA and the UK. Given that Germany and Europe simply cannot compete with the US Internet economy, German industry's goal is to become the capitalist leader and innovator in respect to a different kind of digital technology that makes use of the country's competitive advantage in the export-oriented manufacturing of cars, machinery, chemical and pharmaceutical products, electrical equipment, metals, plastics and rubber products. As part of the Lisbon Strategy, the EU tried to catch up and overtake the USA's world leadership in the development of digital technologies until 2010. This strategy failed. Germany now takes a different approach and wants to digitise and network its manufacturing in order to compete with digital giants such as Google.

Table 5.1 Share of specific industries in total value-added, year 2015 (%)

Industry	USA (%)	UK (%)	Germany (%)
Agriculture, Forestry & Fishery	1.1	0.7	0.6
Manufacturing	12.3	9.8	23.1
Construction	4.2	6.2	4.6
Information & Communication	6.1	6.5	4.7
Finance & Insurance	7.3	7.2	4.1
Real estate	12.5	13.0	10.9
FIRE	19.7	20.2	15.0
Services	78.9	79.9	68.9

Data source: OECD STAN (STructural ANalysis Database).

In the past decades, neoliberal governments, economists, managers, intellectuals and consultants have celebrated the information and communication sector (consisting of industries such as publishing, broadcasting, telecommunications, software and IT services) as the key growth sector. But in Germany (as in other countries), this sector's share of the economy's total value-added only increased from 3.5 per cent in 1991 to 4.7 per cent in 2015 (Table 5.2). Hopes for a new regime of capital accumulation are therefore now shifting from the production of intangible digital information to the production of physical products that have embedded chips and thus blur the boundary between digital and physical systems.

The German manufacturing sector's share in total wages in 2015 was 25.0 per cent, whereas its share in total profits was just 19.6 per cent (Table 5.2). This is an indication that overall manufacturing labour is rather expensive, which puts limits on profitability. At the same time, labour productivity per hour worked has significantly increased since the early 1990s. The Monetary Expression of Labour Time (MELT) measures the relationship of total value in monetary units and total working hours. It is a measure of labour productivity, the total value produced per hour, where total value includes newly created value and transferred value. MELT combines two measures of value – money and labour-time. In German manufacturing, MELT increased from 25.9 euros per hour in 1991 to 59.6 euros per hour in 2016 (source of all data used for the calculations presented in this paragraph is OECD STAN). The total number of hours worked in manufacturing decreased during the same period from 15.2 billion hours to 10.9 billion hours, which meant a reduction of the manufacturing share in total annual working hours in the entire economy from 27.4 per cent to 22.9 per cent. German manufacturing has over a period of 25 years multiplied its productivity by a factor of 2.5 (MELT). The total German economy's MELT increased from 23.8 euros in 1991 to 47.8 euros in 2016. This means that manufacturing's productivity increase has in Germany been significantly higher than the general productivity increase. At the same time, labour compensation as share of total manufacturing value (the wage share in the manufacturing sector) has in 2016 been 60.8 per cent in manufacturing in comparison to a wage share of 56.4 per cent in the total German economy. German manufacturing labour is highly productive and relatively expensive in relation to the total German economy. German capital seems to hope that advancing automation through industry 4.0 technologies will reduce labour costs so that manufacturing profits will in the future make up a higher share of the monetary value produced per hour than they do at the moment. But the big unknown is whether advancing industry 4.0 will not increase fixed constant capital costs (the costs for buying and maintaining digital machines), which could have negative effects on the profit rate if wage costs are not drastically reduced. For German industry, industry 4.0 certainly seems to be the attempt to increase its profits by disempowering and automating manufacturing labour.

Since the start of the new world economic crisis in 2008, German capitalism's general profit rate (the relationship of profits to investments in the total economy) has decreased from 27.4 per cent in 2008 to 24.3 per

Table 5.2 Share of specific German industries in total value-added (V), total profit (p), total labour costs (l), total newly invested constant capital (c) (%)

Industry	V 1991 (%)	V 2015 (%)	p 1991 (%)	p 2015 (%)	l 1991 (%)	l 2015 (%)	c 1991 (%)	c 2015 (%)
Agriculture, Forestry & Fishery	1.2	0.6	1.8	0.7	0.9	0.5	1.7	1.5
Manufacturing	27.4	23.1	19.6	20.3	30.7	25.0	22.1	19.0
Construction	6.0	4.6	4.4	6.4	7.7	5.0	2.0	1.1
FIRE	13.4	15.0	26.0	24.7	5.5	5.3	27.9	32.1
Services	61.9	68.9	71.3	69.5	57.3	67.4	67.5	74.3
Information & Communication	3.5	4.7	3.4	5.8	3.1	4.4	4.8	4.2
ICT Manufacturing & ICT Services	4.4	5.0	4.0	5.5	3.8	4.8	6.0	4.8

Data source: OECD STAN (STructural ANalysis Database).

cent in 2016 (calculation based on data from OECD STAN). Whereas the profit rate in the information and communication sector tends to be well above the general profit rate, the German manufacturing sector's profit rate tends to be well below the general profit rate (Figure 5.2). Given that in Germany the traditional ICT sector's profit rate is high but its overall share of the economy low, it does not yield enough potential for the large-scale accumulation of capital. The German manufacturing sector has a much larger absolute size than the ICT sector, but a low profit rate. Industry 4.0 is an expression of German capital's strategic hope that the digital sector's high profit rate can be transferred to the manufacturing sector and that thereby the general profit rate's fall and squeeze can be overcome.

5.5 TEN REASONS WHY ONE SHOULD BE SCEPTICAL OF INDUSTRY 4.0[2]

First, the complex relations of de-industrialisation and re-industrialisation, technological unemployment and the creation of new jobs is unlikely to

---

2 Critical reflections on and analyses of industry 4.0 include, for example, Brödner (2015), Butollo and Engel (2015), Dörre (2015, 2016), Hirsch-Kreinsen and ten Hompel (2016), Igelsböck et al. (2016), Pfeiffer (2017), Pfeiffer and Suphan (2015).

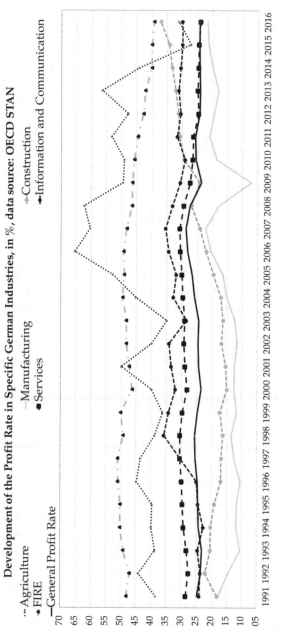

Figure 5.2 The development of the profit rate in Germany

develop in a positive direction under the conditions of capital accumulation and capitalism's inherent structural crisis potentials. Automation is a contradictory process, whose effects are not pre-determined, but shaped by the outcomes of class struggles. There is no doubt that the humanisation of work should involve the automation of dehumanising types of labour, such as the labour of warehouse workers, food packers, toilet cleaners, garbage collectors, electronics and textile assembly line manufacturers and in general any hazardous and monotonous labour. But given the capitalist imperative to increase profit, there is capital's material interest to reduce labour costs and make humans a controllable cog in a (digital) machine, so that the most likely outcome of industry 4.0-based automation under capitalist conditions is an increase of technologically induced unemployment and the human loss of control over the means of production so that digital machines act as means by which capital controls and monitors workers and tries to limit labour's autonomy and decision-power in the production process. Robots do not dissent, do not claim wage increases and better working conditions, do not go on strike and do not work to rule, which makes them interesting for capital as a means to limit the potentials for working class struggles.

The humanisation of labour requires struggles for the autonomy of labour from capital, which must include the control and shaping of digital machines and digital automation. Capital and labour bring opposed interests to the process of automation: Capital wants to reduce labour costs and maximise profits, whereas labour has the interest to maximise the universal and collective control of wealth and production, to minimise toil and realise a good life for all. Digital automation faces in capitalism an antagonism between profit interests and human interests.

It is a standard claim in industry and policy reports about industry 4.0 that robots, algorithms and other digital machines should not control and replace, but assist, relieve and complement human work. But if this idea becomes reality or not is not an abstract idealist question, but one that is embedded into the economy's material interests and struggles. The German manufacturing sector accounted in 2015 for 25.0 per cent of all labour costs, but only for 20.3 per cent of all profits (Table 5.2). German manufacturing is relatively labour-intensive: Whereas the general wage share (the share of wages in value-added) was 56.4 per cent in the total German economy in 2016, it was 60.8 per cent in the manufacturing industry, a value that was higher than in agriculture (45.6 per cent), construction (58.5 per cent), FIRE (20.1 per cent), services (55.6 per cent) and the information and communication sector (53.2 per cent) (calculation based on data from OECD STAN). Given that total wage costs and labour intensity are relatively high in German manufacturing, there is a material interest that German capital tries to use industry 4.0 technologies for replacing human labour and reducing its role in the production process. Because of human labour capacity's complexity, doubts have been raised if it will at all be possible to replace labour in manufacturing to a significant degree by industry 4.0 technologies (Pfeiffer & Suphan 2015). But one should have no doubt that capital's material interest in reducing labour costs in order to increase profits also shapes the introduction of the newest manufacturing technologies. Industry 4.0 is the newest attempt of class struggle from above in the realm of technology.

Second, if production and produced goods become networked over the Internet and embedded into big data flows, then many issues over privacy, data protection and the surveillance of workers and consumers arise. Capital tries to better control workers and consumers via smart technologies and smart goods. *Third*, new risks and complex ethical questions arise: Technological systems are not faultless. Complex technological systems create potentials for accidents and disasters. The less humans are in control, the more difficult it is to avoid disasters in crisis situations. If a self-driving bus that navigates via Google Maps causes an accident with 100 casualties, who is prosecuted? The bus manufacturer? Google? The association that leased the bus for organising an excursion of its members? The failing algorithm? Nobody?

Fourth, if humans are increasingly supported by smart digital machines, then new forms of alienation may emerge: You cannot have a meaningful conversation about life with a robot as you can have with a colleague at work. The behaviour of artificial intelligence systems is to a certain degree unpredictable, which can cause frustration for workers if they cannot achieve their aims by purposive action because a machine makes them act differently in the same type of work situation on different occasions. Such situations can easily occur when smart machines are used because they calculate and oversee numerous context variables that are not visible to and experienceable by the worker.

The next phase of computing requires massive investments that can only be made by large corporations. Therefore, a *fifth* impact can be the advancement of capital concentration and monopolisation. *Sixth*, given that robots can work twenty-four hours, but need at least supervision, questions about working time and work-life balance for humans working with robots arise. *Seventh*, if industry 4.0 is practised as an attempt to de-globalise and bring outsourced production from developing countries back to capitalist core countries, then issues of de-industrialisation may very well affect the Global South and as a consequence global inequalities could further increase.

The total number of the world's employees in the industrial sector has increased from 550 million in 1991 to almost 800 million in 2016 (Table 5.3). Taken together, the number of industrial workers decreased in the developed world during that period from 187 million in 1991 to 160 million in 2016. In the developing world, the number increased from 369 million to 636 million during the same period. Notably, there was an increase from 51.6 million to 125.2 million in India and from 176.2 million to 208.9 million in China. If one of the goals of industry 4.0 is to increase the range of goods manufactured and assembled in Germany and other Western countries, then this could result in de-industrialisation and a loss of industrial jobs in the Global South. The iPad would then no longer be assembled by young, low-paid rural migrants in Chinese Foxconn factories in Shenzen, but by a robot in Munich. For Chinese workers, that would mean downward class mobility from highly exploited industrial workers to becoming unemployed.

Eighth, given that personal transport is one of the main application areas of industry 4.0 (self-driving cars) and fossil fuel continues to be the main energy source of private transport, it is likely that under the regime of fossil capitalism industry 4.0 exacerbates negative environmental impacts. *Ninth*, if the production of physical and other goods becomes networked over the Internet, then new security threats emerge in the context of industrial espionage, hacking, cyber-crime and cyber-terrorism.

Tenth, last but not least, the role of technology in capitalism's crisis tendencies should not be underestimated. In the past decades, the introduction of computerisation has increased fixed capital costs, which in many countries has negatively impacted profit rates, so that capital has advanced wage repression as attempted counter-measure to the tendency of the profit rate to fall. High-tech digital machines are expensive. If this trend continues, then we can expect a new round of attempts to suppress the wage share (the share of the wage sum in the gross domestic product) in order to counter falling profit rates in the context of industry 4.0. Technological hypes have often proven to be mere ideologies that aim at mobilising investments into certain economic sectors, but underestimate

Table 5.3 The development of industrial employment in specific world regions (million), 1991 and 2016

Region	1991	2016
Eastern Europe	57.9	45.1
Northern, Southern and Western Europe	60.9	48.1
USA	31.9	31.6
Canada	3.4	4.1
Australia & New Zealand	2.4	3.2
Japan	22.6	17.3
South Korea	7.1	6.8
Singapore	0.5	0.5
UAE	0.3	2.8
Total developed world	*187.0*	*159.5*
Arab states (without UAE)	3.9	12,1
Northern Africa	9.5	19.9
Sub-Saharan Africa	16.9	46.1
Central and Western Asia	11.3	20.1
South-Eastern Asia and the Pacific (without Australia, New Zealand and Singapore)	28.6	72.4
Latin America and the Caribbean & Mexico	45.5	79.6
Southern Asia	68.9	169.2
Eastern Asia (without Japan and South Korea)	183,6	216,7
Total developing world	*368.2*	*636.1*

Data source: International Labour Organization, World Employment Social Outlook, www.ilo.org/wesodata

capitalism's crisis tendencies. So, for example, the first Internet boom in the mid-1990s resulted in the dot-com crisis in 2000 and the collapse of many Internet corporations. There is much talk about the economic growth potentials of industry 4.0 technologies, but hardly any talk about the impacts on fixed capital costs.

5.6 CONCLUSION: WHY NOT SCHUMPETER, BUT MARX IS THE THEORIST OF THE DIGITAL AGE

Joseph Schumpeter and his theory of long waves are the best ideological friends of the proponents of industry 4.0. They assume with Schumpeter that new technologies have to bring about a new long wave of economic development. But Schumpeter is haunted by Karl Marx's spectre. In

1845/46, Karl Marx and Friedrich Engels wrote *The German Ideology*, in which they criticised some of the main German philosophers of their time, such as Ludwig Feuerbach, Bruno Bauer and Max Stirner, for the neglect of capitalism. 'It has not occurred to any one of these philosophers to inquire into the connection of German philosophy with German reality, the relation of their criticism to their own material surroundings' (Marx & Engels 1845/46: 30).

One hundred and seventy years later, we live in the time of digital capitalism that has created its own peculiar forms of ideology. Industry 4.0 is the new German ideology, the German digital ideology. It has not occurred to any of the consultants and ideologues of industry 4.0 to inquire into the connection of German ideas with German reality, the relation of their ideology to their own material surroundings. They propagate industry 4.0 as the new capitalist panacea, a digital version of God that is said to solve all economic (and other) problems. The actual contradictory class structure of capitalism and its diverging interests are thereby ignored. *The German Ideology* continues by saying that 'the phantoms formed in the human brain are also, necessarily, sublimates of their material life-process, which is empirically verifiable and bound to material premises' (Marx & Engels 1845/46: 36). Industry 4.0 is an ideological phantom formed in the contemporary bourgeoisie's collective brain. It aims at advancing new forms of accumulation, control and class struggle from above.

Marx and Engels argue that whereas German ideology 'descends from heaven to earth, here we ascend from earth to heaven', its critique ascends 'from earth to heaven' by setting out from 'real, active' humans 'on the basis of their real life-process' (Marx & Engels 1845/46: 36). The real life-process of so many today is shaped by precarious labour, social insecurity and inequalities between the rich and the rest. Capitalism is the struggle between capital and humanity. In digital capitalism, capital aims to appropriate digital machines as instruments for political control, economic accumulation and ideological manipulation. Social struggle in digital capitalism is one over the control and shaping of digital machines. Only if humanity appropriates fixed digital capital, turns it and sublates it into a means for the end of humanist socialism and socialist humanism, can we be confident that digital technologies will become disentangled from fetishist and ideological forms (such as industry 4.0) and serve humanity as a whole.

For real wealth is the developed productive power of all individuals. The measure of wealth is then not any longer, in any way, labour time, but rather disposable time. … Just as in the case of an individual, the multiplicity [*Allseitigkeit*] of its [society's] development, its enjoyment and its activity depends on economization of time. Economy of time, to this all economy ultimately reduces itself. (Marx 1857/58: 708, 172–3)

6

Rereading Marx in the Age of Digital Capitalism: Reflections on Michael Hardt and Antonio Negri's Book *Assembly*

6.1 INTRODUCTION

Michael Hardt and Antonio Negri's book *Assembly* is a critical, broad, all-encompassing analysis of contemporary society. It is a major work that turns the trilogy of *Empire* (2000), *Multitude* (2004) and *Commonwealth* (2009) into a tetralogy. These four works are organised around a core of concepts (empire, the multitude, the commons, immaterial labour) that has developed over a period of 17 years in response to capitalism's struggles, contradictions and crises. *Assembly* intervenes into the most recent developments of society and social movements. It asks: 'Why have the movements, which address the needs and desires of so many, not been able to achieve lasting change and create a new, more democratic and just society?' For providing an answer, Hardt and Negri analyse recent changes of politics and the economy.

Assembly focuses on a diversity of interconnected topics such as changes of capitalism, the social production of the commons, digital assemblages, neoliberalism, financialisation, right-wing extremism, protest and political change, political strategies and tactics, social movements and political parties, the entrepreneurship of the multitude, the appropriation of fixed capital, prefigurative politics, taking power differently, antagonistic reformism, political realism or the new Prince. The book offers something interesting for lots of different critical groups and individuals who care about understanding society and changing it towards the better.

The book's main body consists of 295 pages and a ten-page preface organised in 16 chapters and four parts. Parts I and IV ('The Leadership Problem', 'The New Prince') focus on issues of political strategy and tactics, whereas parts II and III ('Social Production', 'Financial Command and Neoliberal Governance') analyse capitalism's transformations. The theoretical approach taken is a critical political economy influenced by Karl Marx, Michel Foucault, Gilles Deleuze, Félix Guattari, Machiavelli and Spinoza.

6.2 CAPITALISM

Hardt and Negri analyse capitalism as a contradictory open totality that in its development has become ever more social and co-operative, but is subject to the dominant class and political elites' control. A dialectic of crises and struggles drives the development of these contradictions.

The social production of the commons that are exploited by capital is a key feature of the contemporary economy and society. 'Today production is increasingly social in a double sense: on one hand, people produce ever more socially, in networks of cooperation and interaction; and, on the other, the result of production is not just commodities but social relations and ultimately society itself' (xv, see also 78).

The common consists for Hardt and Negri of two main forms, the natural and the social commons (166), that are divided into five types: the earth and its ecosystems; the 'immaterial' common of ideas, codes, images and cultural products; 'material' goods produced by co-operative work; metropolitan and rural spaces that are realms of communication, cultural interaction and co-operation; and social institutions and services that organise housing, welfare, health and education (166). Contemporary capitalism's class structure is for Hardt and Negri based on the extraction of the commons, which includes the extraction of natural resources; data mining/data extraction; the extraction of the social from the urban spaces on real estate markets; and finance as extractive industry (166–71).

Hardt and Negri analyse capitalism as having developed in three phases: The phase of primitive accumulation, the phase of manufacture and large-scale industry, and the phase of social production. In chapter 11, they provide a typology of ten features of these three phases. In this analysis, a difference between Hardt/Negri's and David Harvey's approach becomes evident: Whereas Harvey characterises capitalism's imperialistic and exploitative nature based on Rosa Luxemburg as ongoing primitive accumulation, primitive accumulation is for Hardt and Negri a stage of capitalist development. They prefer Marx's notions of formal and real subsumption for characterising capitalism's processes of exploitation and commodification. In an interlude, Hardt and Negri explicitly discuss this difference of their approach to the one by David Harvey (178–82).

David Harvey uses the notions of formal/real subsumption and primitive accumulation in a converse manner to Hardt/Negri: Whereas primitive accumulation is in his theory an ongoing process of accumulation by dispossession, formal and real subsumption characterise two stages in the development of capitalism, one dominated by absolute surplus-value production, the other by relative surplus-value production. Harvey (2017: 117) in his most recent book *Marx, Capital and the Madness of Economic Reason* says that Marx describes a 'move from a formal (coordinations through market mechanisms) to a real (under the direct supervision of capital) subsumption of labour under capital'. 'All the features of primitive accumulation that Marx mentions have remained powerfully present within capitalism's historical geography up until now' (Harvey 2003: 145).

Whereas there are commonalities of Harvey's and Hardt/Negri's analysis of the commons and urban space (see Harvey/Hardt/Negri 2009), it is evident that there are also differences. There is certainly not one correct or valid interpretation of Marx. The decisive circumstance is that Marx 200 years after his birth remains the key influence for understanding capitalism critically. Both Harvey's and Hardt/Negri's works are updates of Marx's theory under the conditions of twenty-first-century capitalism. As long as capitalism exists, people will continue to read Marx in order to find inspiration for how to organise social struggles and will produce new interpretations of Marx. The deep economic crisis of capitalism that has been accompanied by political crises has after decades of postmodernist and neoliberal repression increased the interest in Marx's works.

Another interesting question that Hardt and Negri's *Assembly* poses implicitly is: In what type of capitalism do we live? What dimension of capitalism is dominant? This question has recently also been asked in a debate between Nancy Fraser and Luc Boltanski/Arnaud Esquerre (see Boltanski & Esquerre 2016, 2017; Fraser 2017).

Boltanski and Esquerre suggest the emergence of a new form of cultural capitalism that is based on enrichment from collectibles, luxury goods, brands, arts, heritage, culture, fashion, trends, etc. They speak of the emergence of an integrated capitalism that is based on four forms of valorisation that are based on standardised mass production, the collection form, the trend form and the asset form. Boltanski and Esquerre's approach shows certain parallels to Hardt and Negri's in that both stress that the boundaries of the company and society and between leisure and labour have in the production of value become blurred:

> Work is no longer concentrated in factories and identified as a factor of production; instead, the workforce is widely dispersed, divided between public and private domains, between permanent employees and the informal precariat. It is also spread across a much wider range of activities, many of which are not even identified as 'work', but rather presented as an expression of 'desire' or 'passion', even by those who engage in them, often at heavy cost. (Boltanski & Esquerre 2016: 54)

> Today the divisions of the working day are breaking down as work time and life time are increasingly mixed and we are called on to be productive throughout all times of life. With your smartphone in hand, you are never really away from work or off the clock, and for a growing number of people, constant access not only confuses the boundaries between work and leisure but also eats into the night and sleep. At all hours you can check your e-mail or shop for shoes, read news updates or visit porn sites. The capture of value tends to extend to envelop all the time of life. We produce and consume in a global system that never sleeps. (Hardt & Negri 2017: 185)

Nancy Fraser (2017) argues that Boltanski and Esquerre overestimate cultural capitalism and underestimate finance. In her view, finance capitalism is the dominant form and dimension of capitalism today: 'I worry, ... that Boltanski and Esquerre overestimate enrichment's importance. Perhaps the latter is best understood as an exotic corner of present-day capitalism ... My own candidate for contemporary capitalism's dominant sector is finance. Despite its enormous weight and political consequence, finance receives scant attention from Boltanski and Esquerre' (Fraser 2017: 63).

Hardt and Negri's *Assembly* analyses multiple dimensions of contemporary capitalism: Finance capitalism, neoliberal capitalism and digital/cognitive capitalism. Their analysis suggests that these dimensions interact. Although they do not say it explicitly, there are indications that they see cognitive and digital capitalism as the dominant form and that they therefore are closer to Boltanski and Esquerre than to Fraser in giving an answer to the question in what kind of capitalism we live today: The 'dominant figures of property in the contemporary era – including code, images, cultural products, parents, knowledge, and the like – are largely immaterial and, more important, indefinitely reproducible' (Hardt & Negri 2017: 187).

Many critical theorists will be able to agree that capitalism is a dialectical unity of a diversity of dimensions and forms of capitalism that develop over time so that new aspects emerge, the relevance of certain aspects shifts, etc. (see Fuchs 2014a: chapter 5). My view is that in order to decide which dimension is dominant at a specific point of time, we not only require theory and philosophy, but also need to empirically study various aspects of capitalism, which requires analysing primary and secondary data and applying Marx's theory empirically.

For example, one concrete empirical phenomenon where one can ask what dimensions of capitalism are present is transnational corporations (TNCs). In 2014, 33.5 per cent of the profits of the world's largest 2,000 corporations were located in the finance, insurance and real estate sector, 19.0 per cent in the mobility industries, 18.6 per cent in manufacturing and 17.3 per cent in the information industry (see Fuchs 2016b: table 1). The data suggests that the structure of TNCs is to specific degrees shaped by finance capitalism, mobility capitalism, hyper-industrial capitalism and informational/communicative/digital capitalism.

But all of these dimensions interact: Digital media corporations in Silicon Valley and other parts of the world receive huge injections of venture capital (a specific type of finance capital), aim at becoming listed on stock markets, and are prone to create financial bubbles, as the 2000 dot-com crisis showed. Digital communication advances and is at the same time a result of mobility and time-space compression (Harvey 1989). As a result, the transport of people and commodities has been growing. Digital commodities and digital commons are not weightless, but require not just information work, but also the physical labour of miners and assemblers in Africa and China, who are part of an international division of digital labour (Fuchs 2014a). Finance capitalism, mobility capitalism, hyper-industrial capitalism and digital capitalism form a dialectical capitalist unity that consists of interrelated, contradictory moments. Capitalism is a unity of many capitalisms that develops dynamically and historically. A dimension that makes the picture even more complex is authoritarian capitalism, a form of capitalism that in recent times in the context of the economic and political crisis of capitalism has become strengthened, which poses the question how neoliberal capitalism and authoritarian capitalism are related (Fuchs 2018). Non-trivial questions emerge in this context that need to be addressed from a Marxian perspective: What is authoritarianism? What is authoritarian capitalism? How is it related to fascism, Nazism, right-wing extremism and nationalism? Is Trump an authoritarian personality, an authoritarian capitalist, a right-wing extremist and a neo-fascist? How is the increased prevalence of right-wing extremism, authoritarianism and nationalism related to capitalist development (for a detailed analysis, see Fuchs 2018).

Hardt and Negri stress the importance of the tradition of Western Marxism (72–6), especially Georg Lukács and Maurice Merleau-Ponty, who are representatives of humanist Marxism. The focus on the human subject is indeed a parallel between autonomist Marxism and humanist Marxism. Both are concerned with issues of subjectivity, social change and oppose dogmatic Marxism and Stalinism. Hardt and Negri stress that Merleau-Ponty advanced a 'critique of Soviet dictatorship, which is presented as totalitarianism against subjectivity' (75). One should in this context, however, not forget that the early Merleau-Ponty (1947/1969) in *Humanism and Terror* justified Stalinist terror and defined it as a form of humanism. Later, he clearly moved away from this position and posited humanism against Stalinism.

Hardt and Negri argue that the tendency of the organic composition of capital should not be seen as a deterministic law that results in the breakdown of capitalism, but as a tendency that results in the rise of the general intellect in capitalism (112–14, 203–6) so that 'the general intellect is becoming a protagonist of economic and social production' (114). Such a theoretical move shows the connections between *Das Kapital* and *Die Grundrisse*. There is, therefore, no need to stress 'Marxism against *Das Kapital*' (72). It is much more constructive to focus on the continuities between both books. So, for example, the *Grundrisse*'s notion of general intellect reappears in *Das Kapital* as *allgemeine Arbeit* (general labour), *Gesamtarbeiter* (collective worker) and cognitive and communicative aspects of work (Fuchs 2016d: 30, 36–7, 53–4, 171–2, 192–3, 239–40, 334, 364). Also, class struggle is not alien to *Das Kapital*, but an integral feature that Marx especially discusses in historical passages that focus on struggles about the length and intensity of the working day (see Fuchs 2016d: chapters 10 and 15). It is, therefore, no accident that political readings of *Das Kapital* have also emerged within autonomist Marxism (Cleaver 2000).

6.3 DIGITAL AND COMMUNICATIVE CAPITALISM

Communication and communications have in Marxist theory traditionally been treated as a secondary, superstructural phenomenon of minor importance. As a consequence, the critical theory of communication is today almost entirely associated with Jürgen Habermas' theory of communicative action that advances a dualist ontology that separates work from communication and the economy from the lifeworld (Fuchs 2016a). Hardt and Negri are among those critical theorists who have given serious attention to the analysis of communication and the digital in capitalism. *Assembly* continues in this vein. The decisive point to make is not that everyone should agree with every aspect of their analysis or to claim that digitality is the dominant reality of capitalism, but that Hardt and Negri afford space and time to the analysis of communication and the digital. The analysis of communication and digital communication should not be left to the postmodernists, neoliberals, Habermasians and Luhmannians, but rather be approached from the perspective of Marxist theory (see Fuchs 2008, 2011, 2013, 2014a, 2014b, 2015b, 2016a, 2016d, 2017c; Fuchs & Fisher 2015; Fuchs & Mosco 2016a, 2016b). Hardt and Negri have made an important contribution to the foundations of the emergence of communicative and digital Marxism.

In *Assembly*, Hardt and Negri conceive of the digital as a contradictory realm that poses potentials both for domination and liberation. Digital communication plays a role throughout the entire book and is the specific focus of chapter 7. Although Hardt and Negri do not like the term dialectic, we can say that their analysis of digital communication is a manifestation of a dialectic critical theory of communication that is both opposed to the techno-determinism of techno-optimism and techno-pessimism (see Fuchs 2011: chapter 3 for a detailed discussion of this distinction).

Hardt and Negri oppose their analysis of technology to the approaches of Horkheimer/Adorno and Heidegger, whom they see as techno-pessimists (107–9). There are, however, three important differences between Horkheimer/Adorno and Heidegger:

- For Horkheimer and Adorno, capitalism's instrumental reason is the problem, not technology as such, whereas Heidegger opposes all modern technologies and longs for a pre-modern society without mass media, public transport and electronic communications.

- Adorno did not oppose technology and in less well-known works grounded foundations of an alternative use of contemporary technologies for emancipatory purposes (Fuchs 2016a: chapter 3). A problem of the reception of Horkheimer and Adorno is that there is too much focus on the *Dialectic of the Enlightenment*'s culture industry chapter, which overlooks other works.

- The publication of Heidegger's *Schwarze Hefte* (Black Notebooks) has recently shown that his thought was profoundly anti-Semitic, whereas Adorno was a critical theorist of fascism and anti-Semitism and opposed all fetishistic forms of thought and action (see Fuchs 2015a, 2015c).

Hardt and Negri discern among three phases of modern socio-technological development: automation, digitisation and digital algorithms. In the latter phase, algorithms play a key role in the organisation of exploitation, domination, administration, surveillance and the emergence of digital Taylorism (131–3).

Since 2009, there has been a debate about how to best understand digital prosumption and social media's targeted advertising-based capital accumulation models from a Marxist perspective. Categories such as productive labour, rent, rent-becoming-labour, reproductive labour and unproductive labour have in this context been utilised to the point of theoretical exhaustion (see Fuchs 2014a; Fuchs & Fisher 2015; and especially chapter 5 in Fuchs 2015 for an overview of the most common arguments and counter-arguments in the digital labour debate). Hardt and Negri in *Assembly* take a clear position on these questions: 'Social media too have discovered mechanisms to extract value from the social relationships and connections among users. Behind the value of data, in other words, stands the wealth of social relationships, social intelligence, and social production' (169). 'Those astronomical stock valuations of digital and social media corporations are not just fictional. The corporations have sucked up vast reserves of social intelligence and wealth as fixed capital' (287). The

processes of expropriating value established by such algorithms are also increasingly open and social in a way that blurs the boundaries between work and life. Google users, for instance, are driven by interest and enjoyment, but even without their knowing it, their intelligence, attention, and social relations create value that can be captured. (Hardt & Negri 2017: 119)

Yet exploitation, expropriation and domination are just one side of digital capitalism. Digital technologies are ambivalent and through the contradictory development of the productive forces also advance the socialisation of work and increase the co-operative character of life and society. Hardt and Negri therefore oppose smashing digital machines. They argue for the 'reappropriation of fixed capital, taking back control of the physical machines, intelligent machines, social machines, and scientific knowledges that were created by us in the first place, is one daring, powerful enterprise we could launch in that battle' (120). Appropriating fixed capital 'is not a matter of struggling against or destroying machines or algorithms or any other forms in which our past production is accumulated, but rather wresting them back from capital, expropriating the expropriators, and opening that wealth to society' (287). Hardt and Negri stress the insight that given that technologies are made by humans, they shouldn't be left to capital and the state as tools of domination, but should be transformed into tools of emancipation.

In later chapters of *Assembly*, it becomes evident that when speaking of the appropriation of fixed capital, Hardt and Negri have particularly the leaking of information (e.g. WikiLeaks), open access and the use of digital technologies in protests in mind (128, 214, 273, 294). Hardt and Negri's analysis of the digital as contradictory is a contemporary manifestation of a dialectical analysis of technology. Marx grounded such a theory not just in the *Grundrisse*, but also in *Capital Volume 1*'s chapter on 'Machinery and Large-Scale Industry' (see Fuchs 2016d: chapter 15). We need to add several qualifications to Hardt and Negri's analysis of the digital (see especially Fuchs 2017c):

- The history of alternative media is a history of precarious, self-exploitative labour that has to do with the conundrum that fighting within capitalism against and beyond capitalism requires resources, which are more difficult to obtain when you do not work for-profit, but in self-managed, autonomous co-operatives. We therefore also need left radical reformist media politics that together with media activism advance radical media reforms (such as the taxation of digital advertising and digital corporations, a participatory media fee that redistributes capital and advertising taxation through participatory budgeting to non-profit media, etc.).

• Given the dominance of individualism and the Californian neoliberal ideology in the digital industries and digital culture, there is a real danger that alternative projects (including free software, Wikipedia, WikiLeaks, platform co-ops, network commons, non-commercial open access, etc.) turn into lifestyle politics, individualistic clicktivism, the commodification of the digital commons and a libertarian form of capitalism. Such developments are no automatism, but are a danger that shows the need for political movements that strengthen and struggle for digital commonism.

• Alternative digital media are not limited to progressive, left-wing phenomena such as Alternet, Democracy Now, The Real News, etc. Also the far-right has established its own alternative digital media that act as alternatives to the liberal mainstream media. Some far-right digital media, such as Breitbart and Drudge Report, significantly exceed the popularity, visibility and attention that left-wing digital media achieve. Communication struggles therefore need to not just focus on how to challenge the capitalist mainstream media's power, but also on how to fight against far-right media (Fuchs 2018).

• In the online world, the main power asymmetry does not concern the control of the means of digital production, but the capitalist attention economy: In the flood of information processed at high speed, alternative and critical knowledge is less visible and gains less attention than the content advanced by tabloids, brands, corporations with large advertising budgets, celebrities and entertainment corporations. Appropriating fixed capital, therefore, needs to entail the transformation of the digital towards a new logic that advances engagement, criticality and debate. We, for example, need online equivalents of Club 2,[1] a new form of YouTube that becomes Club 2.0.

• Besides alternative media, there is also a tradition of public service media that to a certain degree resists the logic of commodification and profit, but in many countries is prone to political particular-

---

1 See https://de.wikipedia.org/wiki/Club_2, https://en.wikipedia.org/wiki/After_Dark_ (TV_series).

ism. Just like the Left should take power differently, it should also struggle not just for alternative digital media, but also a public service Internet that transforms the structures of public service media.

6.4 POLITICS

Recent left-wing politics has seen a shift from the politics of occupations to the politics of movement parties. The movements supporting Bernie Sanders and Jeremy Corbyn are the two most striking examples. Reflecting on the question what kind of strategy and tactics today can best advance struggles for a society of the commons, Hardt and Negri oppose one-sided left-wing politics. *Assembly* argues that leaderless horizontality, centralised party politics, prefigurative politics, radical reformism and revolutionary politics all have their limits, problems and pitfalls. Hardt and Negri make arguments for a dialectical politics that combines different forms, strategies and tactics of struggle.

In chapter 4, Hardt and Negri analyse contemporary far-right politics. The aim of contemporary right-wing movements is to 'restore an imagined national identity that is primarily white, Christian, and heterosexual' (50). Hardt and Negri argue that contemporary far-right politics often imitates left-wing movements and are organised as leaderless and structureless movements so that they are different to classical right-wing movements. Donald Trump is arguably the most influential far-right politician today. Trump, who is with one mentioning almost absent in *Assembly*, certainly undermines established party structures. But at the same time he has used money, ideology and popularity to build new structures. And he constitutes a new form of authoritarian, right-wing leadership in which the power of big politics and big capital are fused in one person, the authoritarian spectacle mobilises citizens via reality TV and social media, and a narcissistic self-branding machine engages in constant friend/enemy-politics that takes symbolic political violence to a new level (see Fuchs 2018). Trump is a non-trivial far-right phenomenon that is neither completely new nor completely old, but a development of the strategy and tactics of the far-right.

Hardt and Negri argue both against leaderless horizontality that rejects organisation and institutions and against centralised authority in progressive movements. 'Theoretical investigations, for instance, of the increasingly general intellectual, affective, and communicative capacities of the labor force, sometimes coupled with arguments about the potentials of new media technologies, have been used to bolster the assumption that activists can organize spontaneously and have no need for institutions of any sort' (7). Political leaders of social movements have often been repressed externally by violence and ideology (9) and internally by anti-authoritarianism (9-10). Hardt and Negri also oppose vanguard parties and pure electoral parties. 'Progressive electoral parties, in the opposition and in power, can tactically have positive effects, but as a complement to not a substitute for the movements' (8). They call for an inversion of roles that gives '*strategy to the movements and tactics to the leadership*' (18). They speak of tactical leadership as leadership that is 'limited to short-term action and tied to specific occasions' (19). Hardt and Negri make an argument that social movements should 'strive not to take power as it is but to take power differently' (xiii-xiv). Taking power entails building new institutions beyond representative democracy and building new democratic institutions. The two authors stress the complex relation of centralised Power (potestas/pouvoir/poder/Macht) and power as potential (potentia/puissance/potencia/Vermögen).

Hardt and Negri argue for a political strategy that combines prefigurative politics, antagonistic reformism and taking power to overthrow existing institutions and create new democratic ones (274-80). Employing just one of these forms of politics often faces problems and limits. *Assembly* argues for the complementarity of the three political strategies:

> The taking of power, by electoral or other means, must serve to open space for autonomous and prefigurative practices on an ever-larger scale and nourish the slow transformation of institutions, which must continue over the long term. Similarly practices of exodus must find ways to complement and further projects of both antagonistic reform and taking power. (Hardt & Negri 2017: 278)

Example projects that such a complementary left-wing politics could struggle for include guaranteed basic income as 'a money of the common' (294) and 'open access to and democratic management of the common' (294). Such a form of left-wing politics constitutes a new Machiavellian Prince that does not put Power but the common first (chapter 13).

In more concrete terms, Hardt and Negri argue for a politics of left-wing convergence, in which unions and social movements converge into social unionism that organises social strikes against the exploitation of the social production of the common.

Isn't the left-wing politics that Hardt and Negri argue for a kind of Luxemburgism 2.0 in the age of the social production of the common? Rosa Luxemburg in her time argued against Eduard Bernstein's pure parliamentary social democratic reformism. She opposed anarchist individualism and propagated using the mass strike as political tactic. Luxemburg neither rejected nor fetishished parliamentary politics. She rejected Leninist vanguard party politics and argued for organising the spontaneity of protest. She opposed war, imperialism and nationalism with internationalist politics. She saw that the limitation of democracy in post-revolutionary Russia was a serious shortcoming that would create major problems. Luxemburg argued for dialectics of party/movements, organisation/spontaneity, leader/masses (see Luxemburg 2008). The point where we need to transcend Luxemburg's politics today is that she was very sceptical about the feasibility of autonomous projects, especially co-operatives. Self-management cannot start from nothing in a new society. It needs social forms that germinate in capitalism and produce seeds that as a common point beyond profit and wage-labour.

Hardt and Negri oppose both neoliberal entrepreneurship that resonates 'especially in the digital world of dotcoms and start-ups' (142) and social entrepreneurship that is a 'social neoliberalism' (145) that outsources welfare state to voluntary action, charities and communities. 'The nexus of social neoliberalism and social entrepreneurship destroy community networks and autonomous modes of cooperation that support social life' (146).

Hardt and Negri understand politics as not just taking place on the streets, in factories, squares and offices, but also in the realm of language and communication. They argue that we must politically take and transform the meaning of words and argue that 'transforming words themselves, giving them new meanings' (151) is part of political struggle. 'Sometimes this involves coining new terms but more often it is a matter of taking back and giving new significance to existing ones' (151). 'Indeed one of the central tasks of political thought is to struggle over concepts, to clarify and transform their meaning' (xix).

In this vein, Hardt and Negri argue for transforming the meaning of entrepreneurship. Chapter 9 is dedicated to the 'Entrepreneurship of the Multitude'. 'It is important to claim the concept of entrepreneurship for our own' and not leave it to neoliberal managers and gurus (xix).

By the 'democratic entrepreneurship of the multitude', Hardt and Negri understand the politics of social unionism (social movements + unions) that organises social strikes. Social unions entail 'organizing new social combinations, inventing new forms of social cooperation, generating democratic mechanisms for our access to, use of, and participation in decision-making about the common' (xix). The entrepreneurship of the multitude aims at 'self-organization and self-governance' (146). 'Social unionism ... by combining the organizational structures and innovations of labor unions and social movements, is able to give form to the entrepreneurship of the multitude and the potential for revolt that is inherent in social production' (224).

The transformation of meanings associated with words as political strategy can certainly work for terms such as democracy, freedom, liberty, human rights or the republic. But does it work for the term entrepreneurship? Or the nation? Or capitalism? It would, for example, be absurd and confusing to argue that we need to construct communism as a different capitalism. The word 'capitalism' is so much engrained with the meanings of exploitation and class that trying to appropriate it might very well turn out to be counterproductive. So what about the meaning of entrepreneur, entrepreneurial and entrepreneurialism?

Ernst Bloch suggests fighting the Nazis and fascism should also entail symbolic struggles over words so that communists and socialists appropriate the words that fascists use and give them a different meaning. He argued that the words home and homeland (*Heimat*) should not be left to the fascists, but be used differently: Capitalism alienates humans from society, nature and themselves as their home. Socialism (or what today we could call commonism or a commons-based democracy) is in contrast for Bloch a true homeland that overcomes capitalism and the particularism of nationalist homeland ideology:

> But the root of history is the working, creating human being who reshapes and overhauls the given facts. Once he has grasped himself and established what is his, without expropriation and alienation, in real democracy, there arises in the world something which shines into the childhood of all and in which no one has yet been: homeland. (Bloch 1995: 1375–6)

Hardt and Negri are like Ernst Bloch intransigent optimists, who use the construction of hope as a political weapon in the struggle for alternatives and believe in creating concrete utopias of the common as projects of class struggle. Commonism is a not-yet. The struggles of the multitude are the struggle for realising a political not-yet.

In countries where right-wing extremists win elections and are a major threat, giving a progressive meaning to the terms home and homeland is a feasible political tactic in order to try to win over protest voters who are afraid of social decline. The far-right populist Norbert Hofer almost won the 2016 Austrian presidential election. His party, the Freedom Party (FPÖ), has for many years campaigned against immigration by presenting migrants as a threat to the Austrian homeland. The Freedom Party used election slogans such as 'Heimatliebe statt Marokkaner-Diebe' ('Love of the Homeland instead of Moroccan Thieves') or 'Daham statt Islam' ('Homeland instead of Islam'). The Green Party candidate Alexander Van der Bellen in the 2016 Austrian presidential election appropriated the term homeland and gave a different meaning to it: Social security and solidarity. He won the run-off election against Hofer and became Austrian president. Constructing a different meaning of the word 'home' was used as a linguistic and communicative tactic to counter the threat of far-right politics. His election posters contained slogans such as 'Heimat braucht Zusammenhalt' ('Homeland needs solidarity') or 'Wer unsere Heimat liebt, spaltet sie nicht' ('Those who love our homeland, do not divide it'). Capitalism is an economically divided and alienated society. Racism and nationalism divide society politically and ideologically and are political and ideological forms of alienation. Alienation means that humans are not at home in society because the latter is divided by economic, political and ideological power inequalities. Consequently, the sublation of alienation means to make society humanity's home.

Under specific political conditions, such as the presence of strong right-wing extremist parties, culture jamming, linguistic détournement and semiotic struggle form a feasible method of political struggle. But can the same strategy work for the word entrepreneurship? The term entrepreneur comes from the Old French *entreprendre* that means to undertake and begin something. The term was introduced to the English language in the early nineteenth century. In the world of classical political economy, Jean-Baptiste Say introduced the term of the entrepreneur in the early nineteenth century in his book *A Treatise on Political Economy* (*Traité d'économie politique*) that was first published in 1803: The entrepreneur 'employs, disposes of, and wholly consumes' capital, 'but in a way that reproduces it, and that with profit' (Say 1821/1971: 113). Two hundred years later, the *Encyclopaedia Britannica* understands entrepreneurs as the 'business class' and the entrepreneur as the 'businessman' (Cornwall 2010). It claims that economic growth takes place 'under the leadership of an entrepreneurial class'. Entrepreneurs according to this understanding undertake 'enterprise investment' that aims at the 'growth in labour productivity and GNP' (Cornwall 2010).

Over more than 200 years, the term entrepreneur has been used in an individualistic and capitalistic manner for signifying an individual capitalist who invests and accumulates capital and exploits workers. Is it realistic that now the different political meaning of social unionism can be given successfully to this bourgeois term that signifies individualism and capitalism? There are certain terms that are so corrupted that they should better be discarded than appropriated. It would also not make sense to try to redefine what capitalism is and to give a new meaning to this term. The effect would be that everyone would think one justifies capitalism and does not want to abolish it. We need some words that signify what we oppose. Capitalism and entrepreneurialism are among these negative terms that cannot in a meaningful way undergo a determinate linguistic negation. The risk of appropriating the terms entrepreneur, entrepreneurial and entrepreneurship for progressive purposes is that they are misunderstood as encouraging the commodification of activism. Social unionism is an important political strategy, but it can be called by that name. We do not need a bourgeois category for it. Why do we, for instance, instead of speaking of political entrepreneurship and the entrepreneurship of the multitude, not use as Paolo Gerbaudo (2012) suggests, the terms political choreography and the choreographers of the multitude?

6.5 CONCLUSION

Hardt and Negri's *Assembly* is an important intervention into contemporary politics. The book advances a critical analysis of contemporary capitalism that is shaped by neoliberalism, finance capital, nationalism, right-wing extremism, the common, co-operation, immaterial labour, the digital, algorithms, digital labour, digital assemblages, digital domination and digitally mediated social struggles. Hardt and Negri are ruthless critics of capitalism and bureaucracy as well as intransigent optimists, who care about the next steps in progressive social movement politics.

Assembly argues for rethinking left-wing strategies and tactics. Its authors criticise one-sided approaches and argue for dialectics of movement/leadership, spontaneity/organisation, revolution/reform. The appropriation of fixed capital is an important feature of the suggested strategy and tactics. Hardt and Negri term this politics the new Prince and the entrepreneurship of the multitude.

The key strength of the book is the multitude of dimensions, ideas and provocations that the analysis advances, which makes it a book that will be read by many activists, citizens, scholars and other (im)material workers who care about a better future and are looking for ways to transform society in progressive ways. *Assembly* is a brave and intelligent intervention that will influence our debates, struggles, theories, critiques, praxis, strategies and tactics in the coming years.

7

Conclusion

This book explored how useful Marx's approach, way of thinking and politics are for critically understanding and changing communication, technology and digital media in the twenty-first century.

Chapter 2 showed that it is feasible to read Marx from a media and communication studies perspective. In the twentieth century, the tradition of a critical political economy of communication developed (see Hardy 2014; Mosco 2009). Since the rise of the computer, the Internet and the WWW, this tradition has also been applied to digital media (Fuchs & Dyer-Witheford 2013).

Chapter 3 argued that Marx developed a critical sociology of technology that situates modern technology in the context of capitalism, which allows us to understand, analyse and criticise technology in the context of aspects of dehumanisation, alienation, fixed constant capital, relative surplus-value production, the real subsumption of labour under capital, the antagonism of the productive forces and the relations of production, general intellect, the division of labour, social problems, antagonisms. Marx's approach allows us to situate technology in the context of class struggles against capitalist rule and for a commons-based society.

Chapter 4 pointed out that Marx's approach helps us in grounding foundations of a critical theory of communication. Such a theory stresses that communication is a material, social, societal, economic and non-economic, dialectical process. In the analysis of capitalism and communication, such an approach gives particular attention to the role of the means of communication, ideology, fetishism, knowledge and communicative labour, political communication, global communication in capitalism as well as to struggles for alternative, democratic communications.

Chapter 5 presented a case study of how to apply Marxian analysis to industry 4.0 technologies. These are technologies that combine the Internet of Things, big data, social media, cloud computing, sensors, artificial intelligence and robotics in the production, distribution and use of physical goods. Especially in Germany there are big hopes for the positive and transformative effects of industry 4.0 and the bourgeoisie has for that purpose called out the fourth industrial revolution. The chapter showed that industry 4.0 is predominantly an ideology that aims at new forms of automation in the manufacturing sector in order to reduce labour costs. The industrial bourgeoisie thereby hopes to increase manufacturing's profit rate.

Chapter 6 discussed Michael Hardt and Antonio Negri's book *Assembly*. Among certain Marxists, it has become fashionable to write papers against Hardt and Negri and dismiss their approach. Although one certainly can have criticism of other approaches, the critique of Hardt and Negri seems to be often motivated by envy, sectarianism and orthodoxy. One of their achievements that should be acknowledged is that they have continuously stressed and reminded others that digital capitalism is one of the important dimensions of contemporary capitalist society.

The five chapters of this book were written in different contexts, but share the overall purpose to show that Marx's works are not outdated, but form an important intellectual means of struggle that empowers our critical interpretation capacities of digital capitalism. Such capacities are needed as one of the foundations of struggles for communicative socialism and digital commonism.

Karl Marx has frequently been pronounced dead. Bourgeois and postmodern intellectuals have again and again stressed that Marx's theory is outdated, reductionist, deterministic, totalitarian, etc. In reality, Marx's approach is topical, dialectical and democratic. Whereas bourgeois critics of Marx aim at silencing any critique of capitalism, postmodern critics tend to think that identity politics is more important than class politics and that the latter no longer counts today.

Socio-economic inequalities and the economic crisis of capitalism that started in 2008 have made evident that Marx's approach is highly topical today. Although his remains are buried in Highgate Cemetery, Marx is not dead as long as capitalism is alive. That Marx is alive means that the need for the critique of capitalism and class is needed. Such a critique is always a dialectical critique, which means it is relational, dynamic, materialist and a class struggle perspective.

Rereading and repeating Marx certainly means renewing the critical theory of capitalism and class. Marx's theory and theoretical approaches building on it necessarily have a focus on capitalism and class. But whereas bourgeois and postmodern theories have simply ignored capitalism and class, a contemporary Marxist theory should not make the mistake to only talk about capitalism and class without mediations.

This book has shown that rereading Marx can inspire our critical thinking on technology, communication, automation, digital technologies and digital/communicative capitalism. Analysing such phenomena from a Marxian perspective requires that we relate them to the analysis of class struggles, power and capitalism. Marx had interesting things to say on communication and technologies that can form one of the foundations of a critical theory of communication and technology.

Rereading Marx does not assume that capitalism has not change since the nineteenth century when Marx was writing his works. It is often claimed that Marx's analysis is limited to nineteenth-century British capitalism and is therefore outdated when it comes to the analysis of contemporary twenty-first-century society. But Marx's dialectical methodology and dialectical theory is not just a dialectical logic, but also a dialectical concept of history. Society changes through crises and human practices such as revolutions. Marx did not assume that society never changes, but rather argued that society is shaped by a dialectic of change and continuity. Digital and communicative capitalism has the same foundational structures as nineteenth-century capitalism. But these foundational structures are expressed in new ways and forms. Twenty-first-century capitalism is neither completely different from nor completely identical with nineteenth-century capitalism.

When we speak of digital and communicative capitalism then we mean a tendency and dimension of contemporary capitalisms. Capitalism is many capitalisms at the same time that are interconnected: finance capitalism, digital/communicative capitalism, mobility capitalism, hyper-industrial capitalism, etc. So, for example, large digital media corporations in the USA often receive injections by venture capital and are listed and traded on financial markets, which indicates an interconnection of finance capitalism and digital capitalism.

Marx's dialectics is an important tool of thought and practice for thinking about communication, technology and the digital today. It allows us to conceive of communication, technology and the digital in terms of contradictions. One can thereby avoid technological and other forms of determinism, reductionism, individualism, structuralism, relativism, etc. Marx's approach is practical in that it stresses that in antagonistic societies, class and social struggles are decisive factors that influence development. Besides praxis as subjective factor there are also objective crisis tendencies that influence development. Society's development is shaped by a dialectic of subject and object. The objective antagonisms of society condition social struggles that in turn condition the development of society's antagonisms.

Reading Marx today can inspire us to make sense of and criticise contemporary capitalist societies that to a significant degree depend on communication technologies, digital technologies, knowledge labour, digital labour, ideology, the commodification of the commons and social relations. Such a rereading can inspire not just analyses of capitalist society, but also social struggles that aim at transcending capitalism, exploitation, class and domination. The commons-based society that Marx envisaged is a participatory democracy. Engaging with aspects of communication and technology based on Marx allows us to understand the contradictory character of communicative/digital capitalism and to envision ways towards communicative socialism and digital commonism.

Bibliography

Websites last accessed 27 April 2019.

Aichholzer, Georg, Niklas Gudowsky, Florian Saurwein et al. 2015. *Industrie 4.0. Foresight & Technkfolgenabschätzung zur gesellschaftlichen Dimension der nächsten industriellen Revolution. Zusammenfassender Endbericht*. Wien: Österreichische Akademie der Wissenschaften.

Andrejevic, Mark. 2007. *iSpy: Surveillance and Power in the Interactive Era*. Lawrence, KS: University Press of Kansas.

Austrian Institute of Technology, WIFO & Fraunhofer Austria Research. 2017. *Beschäftigung und Industrie 4.0*. Wien: Bundesministerium für Verkehr, Innovation und Technologie.

Barbrook, Richard. 2007. *Imaginary Futures*. London: Pluto Press.

Bell, Daniel. 1976. *The Coming of Post-Industrial Society*. New York: Basic Books.

Bitkom. 2015. *Umsetzungsstrategie Industrie 4.0. Ergebnisbericht der Plattform Industrie 4.0*. Berlin: Bitkom.

Bloch, Ernst. 1995. *The Principle of Hope. Volume Three*. Cambridge, MA: MIT Press.

Boltanski, Luc and Arnaud Esquerre. 2016. The Economic Life of Things. Commodities, Collectibles, Assets. *New Left Review* 98: 31–54.

Boltanski, Luc and Arnaud Esquerre. 2017. Enrichment, Profit, Critique. A Rejoinder to Nancy Fraser. *New Left Review* 106: 67–76.

Braverman, Harry. 1974/1998. *Labor and Monopoly Capital. The Degradation of Work in the Twentieth Century*. New York: Monthly Review Press.

Brödner, Peter. 2015. Industrie 4.0 und Big Data. Kritik einer technikzentrierten Perspektive. *Z – Zeitschrift Marxistische Erneuerung* 103: 75–84.

Buhr, Manfred and Alfred Kosing.1979. *Kleines Wörterbuch der Marxistisch-Leninistischen Philosophie*. Opladen: Westdeutscher Verlag. Fourth edition.

Bundesminsterium für Arbeit und Soziales. 2015. *Grünbuch Arbeiten 4.0*. Berlin: Bundesminsterium für Arbeit und Soziale.

Bundesministerium für Bildung und Forschung. 2013. *Zukunftsbild 'Industrie 4.0'*. Bonn: Bundesministerium für Bildung und Forschung.

Bundesministerium für Wirtschaft und Energie. 2015. *Industrie 4.0. Volks- und betriebswirtschaftliche Faktoren für den Standort Deutschland. Eine Studie im Rahmen der Begleitforschung zum Technologieproramm AUTONOMIK für Industrie 4.0*. Berlin: Bundesministerium für Wirtschaft und Energie.

Butollo, Florian and Thomas Engel. 2015. Industrie 4.0 – arbeits- und gesellschaftspolitische Perspektiven. *Z – Zeitschrift Marxistische Erneuerung* 103: 29–41.

Cleaver, Harry. 2000. *Reading Capital Politically*. Leeds: Anti/Theses.

Consalvo, Mia and Charles Ess (eds). 2012. *The Handbook of Internet Studies.* Oxford: Wiley-Blackwell.

Cornwall, John L. 2010. Economic Growth. In *Encyclopaedia Britannica Online.* www.britannica.com/topic/economic-growth

Dean, Jodi. 2010. *Blog Theory.* Cambridge: Polity.

Dörre, Klaus. 2015. Digitalisierung – Neue Prosperität oder Vertiefung gesellschaftlicher Spaltungen? In Hartmut Hirsch-Kreinsen, Peter Ittermann and Jonathan Niehaus (eds), *Digitalisierung industrieller Arbeit: Die Vision Industrie 4.0 und ihre sozialen Herausforderungen,* pp. 269–84. Baden-Baden: Nomos.

—— 2016. Industrie 4.0 – Neue Prosperität oder Vertiefung gesellschaftlicher Spaltungen? DFG-KollegforscherInnengruppe Postwachstumsgesellschaften Working Paper 02/2016. Jena: Universität Jena.

Dyer-Witheford, Nick. 1999. *Cyber-Marx. Cycles and Circuits of Struggle in High-Technology Capitalism.* Urbana, IL: University of Illinois Press.

—— 2015. *Cyber-Proletariat: Global Labour in the Digital Vortex.* London: Pluto Press.

Dyer-Witheford, Nick and Greig De Peuter. 2009. *Games of Empire: Global Capitalism and Video Games.* Minneapolis, MN: University of Minnesota Press.

Eagleton, Terry. 2011. *Why Marx Was Right.* New Haven, CT: Yale University Press.

—— 2013. Why I Never Use Email. *Prospect Magazine,* July. www.prospectmagazine.co.uk/magazine/terry-eagleton-email-internet

Fisher, Eran. 2010. *Media and New Capitalism in the Digital Age.* Basingstoke: Palgrave Macmillan.

Fornäs, Johan. 2013. *Capitalism: A Companion to Marx's Economy Critique.* London: Routledge.

Forschungsunion Wirtschaft – Wissenschaft & Deutsche Akademie der Technikwissenschaften. 2013. *Umsetzungsempfehlungen für das Zukunftsprojekt Industrie 4.0.* Frankfurt am Main: Plattform Industrie 4.0.

Fraser, Nancy. 2017. A New Form of Capitalism? A Reply to Boltanski and Esquerre. *New Left Review* 106: 57–65.

Fuchs, Christian. 2008. *Internet and Society: Social Theory in the Information Age.* New York: Routledge.

—— 2011. *Foundations of Critical Media and Information Studies.* Abingdon: Oxon.

—— 2012. Towards Marxian Internet Studies. *tripleC: Communication, Capitalism & Critique* 10 (2): 392–412.

—— 2013. Why and How to Read Marx's 'Capital'? Reflections on Johan Fornäs' Book 'Capitalism. A Companion to Marx's Economy Critique'. *tripleC: Communication, Capitalism & Critique* 11 (2): 294–309.

—— 2014a. *Digital Labour and Karl Marx.* New York: Routledge.

—— 2014b. *OccupyMedia! The Occupy Movement and Social Media in Crisis Capitalism.* Winchester: Zero Books.

—— 2015a. Anti-Semitism, Anti-Marxism, and Technophobia: The Fourth Volume of Martin Heidegger's *Black Notebooks* (1942–1948). *tripleC: Communication, Capitalism & Critique* 13 (1): 93–100.

—— 2015b. *Culture and Economy in the Age of Social Media.* New York: Routledge.

—— 2015c. Martin-Heidegger's Anti-Semitism: Philosophy of Technology and the Media in the Light of the 'Black Notebooks'. Implications for the Reception of Heidegger in Media and Communication Studies. *tripleC: Communication, Capitalism & Critique* 13 (1): 55–78.

—— 2016a. *Critical Theory of Communication. New Readings of Lukács, Adorno, Marcuse, Honneth and Habermas in the Age of the Internet.* London: University of Westminster Press.

—— 2016b. Digital Labor and Imperialism. *Monthly Review* 67 (8): 14–24.

—— 2016c. Henryk Grossmann 2.0: A Critique of Paul Mason's Book 'Post-Capitalism: A Guide to Our Future'. *tripleC: Communication, Capitalism & Critique* 14 (1): 232–43.

—— 2016d. *Reading Marx in the Information Age: A Media and Communication Studies Perspective on Capital Volume 1.* New York: Routledge.

—— 2017a. Preface: Horst Holzer's Marxist Theory of Communication. *tripleC: Communication, Capitalism & Critique* 15 (2): 686–725.

—— 2017b. Raymond Williams' Communicative Materialism. *European Journal of Cultural Studies* 20 (6): 744–62.

—— 2017c. *Social Media: A Critical Introduction.* London: Sage. Second edition.

—— 2018. *Digital Demagogue: Authoritarian Capitalism in the Age of Trump and Twitter.* London: Pluto Press.

—— 2019. Henri Lefebvre's Theory of the Production of Space and the Critical Theory of Communication. *Communication Theory.*

Fuchs, Christian and Nick Dyer-Witheford. 2013. Karl Marx@Internet Studies. *New Media & Society* 15 (5): 782–96.

Fuchs, Christian and Eran Fisher (eds). 2015. *Reconsidering Value and Labour in the Digital Age.* Basingstoke: Palgrave Macmillan.

Fuchs Christian and Vincent Mosco (eds). 2012. Special Issue: Marx is Back: The Importance of Marxist Theory and Research for Critical Communication Studies Today. *tripleC: Communication, Capitalism & Critique* 10 (2): 127–632.

Fuchs, Christian and Vincent Mosco (eds). 2016a. *Marx and the Political Economy of the Media.* Leiden: Brill.

Fuchs, Christian and Vincent Mosco (eds). 2016b. *Marx in the Age of Digital Capitalism.* Leiden: Brill.

Gerbaudo, Paolo. 2012. *Tweets and the Streets. Social Media and Contemporary Activism.* London: Pluto Press.

Golding, Peter and Graham Murdock (eds). 1997. *The Political Economy of the Media.* 2 Volumes. Cheltenham: Edward Elgar.

Gorz, André. 1982. *Farewell to the Working Class: An Essay on Post-Industrial Socialism.* London: Pluto Press.

—— 1989. *Critique of Economic Reason.* London: Verso.

Grossmann, Henryk. 1929/1992. *The Law of Accumulation and Breakdown of the Capitalist System. Being Also a Theory of Crises.* London: Pluto Press.

Hardt, Michael and Antonio Negri. 2000. *Empire.* Cambridge, MA: Harvard University Press.

Hardt, Michael and Antonio Negri. 2004. *Multitude: War and Democracy in the Age of Empire.* New York: Penguin.

Hardt, Michael and Antonio Negri. 2009. *Commonwealth.* Cambridge, MA: Harvard University Press.

Hardt, Michael and Antonio Negri. 2017. *Assembly.* Oxford: Oxford University Press.

Hardy, Jonathan. 2014. *Critical Political Economy of the Media: An Introduction.* London: Routledge.

Harvey, David. 1982/2006. *The Limits to Capital.* London: Verso.

—— 1989. *The Condition of Postmodernity. An Enquiry into the Origins of Cultural Change.* Oxford: Blackwell.

—— 2001. *Spaces of Capital. Towards a Critical Geography.* New York: Routledge.

—— 2003. *The New Imperialism.* Oxford: Oxford University Press.

—— 2005. *A Brief History of Neoliberalism.* Oxford: Oxford University Press.

—— 2010. *A Companion to Marx's Capital.* London: Verso.

—— 2012. *Rebel Cities. From the Right to the City to the Urban Revolution.* London: Verso.

—— 2013. *A Companion to Marx's Capital Volume 2.* London: Verso.

—— 2014. *Seventeen Contradictions and the End of Capitalism.* Oxford: Oxford University Press.

—— 2017. *Marx, Capital and the Madness of Economic Reason.* London: Profile Books.

Harvey, David, Michael Hardt and Antonio Negri. 2009. *Commonwealth:* An Exchange. *Artforum* 48 (3): 210–21.

Hegel, Georg Wilhelm Friedrich. 1991. *The Encyclopaedia Logic (with the Zusätze). Part I of the Encyclopaedia of Philosophical Sciences with the Zusätze.* Indianapolis, IN: Hackett.

Heinrich, Michael. 2012. *An Introduction to the Three Volumes of Karl Marx's Capital.* New York: Monthly Review Press.

—— 2013. Crisis Theory, the Law of the Tendency of the Profit Rate to Fall, and Marx's Studies in the 1870s. *Monthly Review* 64 (11): 15–31.

—— 2014. The 'Fragment on Machines': A Marxian Misconception in the *Grundrisse* and its Overcoming in *Capital*. In Riccardo Bellofiore, Guido Starosta and Peter D. Thomas (eds), *In Marx's Laboratory. Critical Interpretations of the Grundrisse*, pp. 197–212. Chicago, IL: Haymarket.

Hirsch-Kreinsen, Hartmut and Michael ten Hompel. 2016. Digitalisierung industrieller Arbeit. Entwicklungsperspektiven und Gestaltungsansätze. In Birgit Vogel-Heuser, Thomas Bauernhansel and Michael ten Hompel (eds), *Handbuch Industrie 4.0: Produktion, Automatisierung und Logistik*, pp. 1–20. Berlin: Springer.

Holtgrewe, Ursula, Thomas Riesenecker-Caba and Jörg Flecker. 2015. 'Industrie 4.0' – eine arbeitssoziologische Einschätzung. Endbericht für die AK Wien. Wien: FORBA.

Holzer, Horst. 1975. Theorie des Fernsehens: Fernseh-Kommunikation in der Bundesrepublik Deutschland. Hamburg: Hoffmann und Campe.

Huws, Ursula. 2003. The Making of a Cybertariat. Virtual Work in a Real World. New York: Monthly Review Press.

—— 2015. Labor in the Global Digital Economy: The Cybertariat Comes of Age. New York: Monthly Review Press.

Igelsböck, Judith, Irina Koprax, Martin Kuhlmann, Karin Link and Clemens Zierler. 2016. Bestandsaufnahme Arbeitspolitik in Oberösterreich: Herausforderungen und Perspektiven im Kontext von Industrie 4.0 und veränderten Marktanforderungen. Linz: Institut für Arbeitsforschung und Arbeitspolitik an der Johannes Kepler Universität Linz.

Jameson, Frederic. 2011. Representing Capital: A Reading of Volume One. London: Verso.

Jhally, Sut. 2006. The Spectacle of Accumulation. Essays in Culture, Media, & Politics. New York: Peter Lang.

Kliman Andrew, Alan Freeman, Nick Potts, Alexey Gusey and Brendan Cooney. 2013. The Unmaking of Marx's Capital: Heinrich's Attempt to Eliminate Marx's Crisis Theory. SSRN Working Papers Series 22, July. http://mpra.ub.uni-muenchen.de/48535/1/MPRA_paper_48535.pdf

Kofler, Leo. 1970. Marxismus und Sprache. In Stalinismus und Bürokratie, pp. 115–82. Neuwied am Rhein: Luchterhand.

Lent, John and Michelle Amazeen (eds). 2015. Key Thinkers in Communication Scholarship. New York: Palgrave Macmillan.

Lukács, Georg. 1986a. Zur Ontologie des gesellschaftlichen Seins. Erster Halbband Bände. Georg Lukács Werke, Band 13. Darmstadt: Luchterhand.

—— 1986b. Zur Ontologie des gesellschaftlichen Seins. Zweiter Halbband Bände. Georg Lukács Werke, Band 14. Darmstadt: Luchterhand.

Luxemburg, Rosa. 1916. The Junius Pamphlet: The Crisis in the German Social Democracy. In Mary-Alice Waters (ed.), Rosa Luxemburg Speaks, pp. 371–477. New York: Pathfinder.

—— 1976. The National Question: Selected Writings. New York: Monthly Review Press.

—— 2008. The Essential Rosa Luxemburg. Chicago, IL: Haymarket.

Marcuse, Herbert. 1968/2009. Negations: Essays in Critical Theory. London: MayFly.

Marx, Karl. 1842. Proceedings of the Sixth Rhine Province Assembly. First Article. Debates on Freedom of the Press and Publication of the Proceedings of the Assembly of the Estates. In Marx & Engels Collected Works (MECW) Volume 1, pp. 132–81. London: Lawrence & Wishart.

—— 1844a. Comments on James Mill's 'Elements of Political Economy'. In Marx & Engels Collected Works (MECW) Volume 3, pp. 211–28. London: Lawrence & Wishart.

—— 1844b. Contribution to the Critique of Hegel's Philosophy of Law. Introduction. In *Marx & Engels Collected Works (MECW) Volume 3*, pp. 175–87. London: Lawrence & Wishart.

—— 1844c. Economic and Philosophic Manuscripts of 1844. In *Marx & Engels Collected Works (MECW) Volume 3*, pp. 229–346. London: Lawrence & Wishart.

—— 1845/46. Theses on Feuerbach. In *Marx & Engels Collected Works (MECW) Volume 5*, pp. 3–5. London: Lawrence & Wishart.

—— 1847. Wages. In *Marx & Engels Collected Works (MECW) Volume 6*, pp. 415–37. London: Lawrence & Wishart.

—— 1848. Reply of Frederick William IV to the Delegation of the Civic Militia. In *Marx & Engels Collected Works (MECW) Volume 7*, pp. 476–7. London: Lawrence & Wishart.

—— 1857/58. *Grundrisse*. London: Penguin.

—— 1859. A Contribution to the Critique of Political Economy. In *Marx & Engels Collected Works (MECW) Volume 29*, pp. 257–507. London: Lawrence & Wishart.

—— 1861–63. Economic Manuscript of 1861–63 (Conclusion). In *Marx & Engels Collected Works (MECW) Volume 34*. London: Lawrence & Wishart.

—— 1864. Inaugural Address of the Working Men's International Association. In *Marx & Engels Collected Works (MECW) Volume 20*, pp. 5–13. London: Lawrence & Wishart.

—— 1865. Value, Price and Profit. In *Marx & Engels Collected Works (MECW) Volume 20*, pp. 101–49. London: Lawrence & Wishart.

—— 1867. *Capital Volume 1*. London: Penguin.

—— 1870. Letter of Marx to Sigfrid Meyer and August Vogt, 9 April 1870. In *Marx & Engels Collected Works (MECW) Volume 43*, pp. 471–6. London: Lawrence & Wishart.

—— 1881. Marginal Notes on Adolph Wagner's 'Lehrbuch der Politischen Ökonomie'. In *Marx & Engels Collected Works (MECW) Volume 24*, pp. 531–59. London: Lawrence & Wishart.

—— 1885. *Capital Volume 2*. London: Penguin.

—— 1894. *Capital Volume 3*. London: Penguin.

—— 1964. *Frammento sulle macchine*. Translated by Renato Solmi. *Quaderni Rossi* 4: 289–300.

—— 1963. *Theories of Surplus Value. Part 1*. London: Lawrence & Wishart.

—— 1969. *Theories of Surplus Value. Part 2*. London: Lawrence & Wishart.

—— 1972. *Theories of Surplus Value. Part 3*. London: Lawrence & Wishart.

Marx, Karl and Friedrich Engels. 1845/46. The German Ideology. In *Marx & Engels Collected Works (MECW) Volume 5*, pp. 19–539, London: Lawrence & Wishart.

Mason, Paul. *PostCapitalism: A Guide to Our Future*. London: Allen Lane.

Mattelart Armand and Seth Siegelaub (eds). 1979. *Communication and Class Struggle. Volume 1: Capitalism, Imperialism*. New York: International General.

Mattelart Armand and Seth Siegelaub (eds). 1983. *Communication and Class Struggle. Volume 2: Liberation, Socialism.* New York: International Mass Media Research Center.

MECW: Marx, Karl and Friedrich Engels. *Marx & Engels Collected Works (MECW).* 50 Volumes. London: Lawrence & Wishart.

Mehring, Franz. 1918. Karl Marx. In *Franz Mehring Gesammelte Schriften Band 4: Aufsätze zur Geschichte der Arbeiterbewegung,* pp. 11–15. Berlin: Dietz.

—— 1936/2003. *Karl Marx: The Story of His Life.* Abingdon: Routledge.

Meisner, Matthias. 2013. Das Kapital ist Unesco-Welterbe: Linke nicht nur froh über Marx als Bestseller. *Der Tagesspiegel Online,* 20 June. www.tagesspiegel.de/politik/das-kapital-ist-unesco-welterbe-linke-nicht-nur-froh-ueber-marx-als-bestseller/8382050.html

Merleau-Ponty, Maurice. 1947/1969. *Humanism and Terror. An Essay on the Communist Problem.* Boston, MA: Beacon Press.

MEW: Marx, Karl and Friedrich Engels. *Marx Engels Werke (MEW).* 44 Volumes. Berlin: Dietz.

Moore Phoebe and Athina Karatzogianni (eds). 2009. Parallel Visions of Peer Production. *Capital & Class* 33 (1): 7–177.

Mosco, Vincent. 2004. *The Digital Sublime.* Cambridge, MA: MIT Press.

—— 2009. *The Political Economy of Communication.* London: Sage. Second edition.

—— 2014. *To the Cloud. Big Data in a Turbulent World.* Boulder, CO: Paradigm.

Murdock, Graham and Peter Golding. 1973. For a Political Economy of Mass Communications. *Socialist Register* 10: 205–34.

Negri, Antonio. 1991. *Marx Beyond Marx. Lessons on the Grundrisse.* New York: Autonomedia.

Noble, David F. 1984/2011. *Forces of Production: A Social History of Industrial Automation.* New Brunswick, NJ: Transaction Publishers. Second edition.

—— 1995. *Progress Without People. New Technology, Unemployment, and the Message of Resistance.* Toronto: Between the Lines.

Pfeiffer, Sabine. 2017. The Vision of 'Industrie 4.0' in the Making – a Case of Future Told, Tamed, and Traded. *Naonoethics* 11: 107–21.

Pfeiffer, Sabine and Anne Suphan. 2015. Der AV-Index. Lebendiges Arbeitsvermögen und Erfahrung als Ressourcen auf dem Weg zu Industrie 4.0. Universität Hohenheim Lehrstuhl für Soziologie Working Paper 2015/1. Hohenheim: Universität Hohenheim.

Pollock, Frederick. 1957. *Automation: A Study of its Economic and Social Consequences.* New York: Praeger.

Qiu, Jack. 2016. *Goodbye iSlave. A Manifesto for Digital Abolition.* Urbana, IL: University of Illinois Press.

Rosdolsky, Roman. 1977. *The Making of Marx's 'Capital'. Volume 1.* London: Pluto Press.

Rossi-Landi, Ferruccio. 1983. *Language as Work and Trade. A Semiotic Homology for Linguistics & Economics.* South Hadley, MA: Bergin & Garvey.

Rovatti, Pier Aldo. 1973. The Critique of Fetishism in Marx's *Grundrisse. Telos* 17: 56–69.

Say, Jean-Baptiste. 1821/1971. *A Treatise on Political Economy*. New York: Kelley.

Schiller, Dan. 2000. *Digital Capitalism*. Cambridge, MA: MIT Press.

Smythe, Dallas W. 1977. Communications: Blindspot of Western Marxism. *Canadian Journal of Political and Social Theory* 1 (3): 1–27.

Söderberg, Johan. 2008. *Hacking Capitalism*. New York: Routledge.

Spath, Dieter, Oliver Ganschar, Stefan Gerlach, Moritz Hämeerle, Tobias Krause and Sebastian Schlund. 2013. *Produktionsarbeit der Zukunft – Industrie 4.0*. Stuttgart: Fraunhofer Verlag.

Srnicek, Nick and Alex Williams. 2015. *Inventing the Future. Postcapitalism and a World Without Work*. London: Verso.

Stalin, Joseph V. 1913. Marxism and the National Question. In *Stalin Works Volume 2*, pp. 300–81. Moscow: Foreign Languages Publishing House.

—— 1972. *Marxism and the Problems of Linguistics*. Peking: Foreign Languages Press.

Sum, Ngai-Ling and Bob Jessop. 2013. *Towards a Cultural Political Economy: Putting Culture in its Place in Political Economy*. Cheltenham: Edward Elgar.

Vercellone, Carlo. 2007. From Formal Subsumption to General Intellect: Elements for a Marxist Reading of the Thesis of Cognitive Capitalism. *Historical Materialism* 15 (1): 13–36.

Virno, Paolo. 1996. Notes on the 'General Intellect'. In Saree Makdisi, Cesare Casarino and Rebecca E. Karl (eds), *Marxism Beyond Marxism*, pp. 265–72. New York: Routledge.

Wark, McKenzie. 2004. *A Hacker Manifesto*. Cambridge, MA: Harvard University Press.

Wasko, Janet. 2014. The Study of Political Economy of the Media in the Twenty-First Century. *International Journal of Media & Cultural Politics* 10 (3): 259–71.

Wasko Janet, Graham Murdock and Helena Sousa (eds). 2011. *The Handbook of Political Economy of Communications*. Malden, MA: Wiley-Blackwell.

Williams, Raymond. 1977. *Marxism and Literature*. Oxford: Oxford University Press.

—— 1980. Advertising: The Magic System. In *Culture and Materialism*, pp. 170–94. London: Verso.

—— 1989. *What I Came to Say*. London: Hutchinson Radius.

Index